vol. 1

THE MOLEHILL: VOLUME ONE
© 2012 Rabbit Room Press
Published with care and diligence by:
RABBIT ROOM PRESS
523 Heather Place
Nashville, Tennessee 37204
info@rabbitroom.com

Edited by Pete Peterson
Additional editing by Jonathan Rogers
Cover concept, illustration & design by C. Stewart (cstewartstudio.com)

Warning: Do not place this book within reach of a vole. They are impostors not to be trusted. They don't even have hills.

ISBN 978-0-9826214-9-3
FIRST EDITION
Printed in the United States of America
12 13 14 15 16 17— 6 5 4 3 2 1

RABBIT ROOM
— P R E S S —

the
MOLEHILL

volume 1

e collibus montes

Contents

Say You, Say Molehill

by A. S. Peterson, Editor

Several years ago a good friend, aspiring curmudgeon Jonathan Rogers, stabbed his bony finger my way, stepped onto his well-worn soapbox, and proclaimed: "It's time the Rabbit Room stopped talking about culture and started creating it!" I've forgotten what happened next, but I'll bet it involved either a waffle or an alligator.

A few months later I started to think seriously about assembling a sort of Rabbit Room annual. We made our first go of it thinking that maybe we could get off as easily as dredging up old posts from the website, polishing them off, and binding them in a shiny cover. It would be like a greatest hits record, we thought—only in book form, and with old blog posts. This idea died a deservedly miserable death.

But attempting that "greatest hits" idea did have its uses in the end. We went through all of our posts (over a thousand) and pulled out the cream of the crop—those we felt were the best written, or were the most important, or didn't get the attention they deserved. And when I'd collected all those chart-toppers together, I began editing. That's when the real flaw in the plan revealed itself.

What we hadn't considered was growth. The Rabbit Room has been around in some form since 2006, and in the four intervening years, we had all become better writers. When I looked at those old posts, what I saw was a herd of greenhorns trying to find their way—I saw underdeveloped ideas, poorly structured essays, horrific punctuation, a heck of a lot of adverbs, and a rat's nest of aimless meta-phors. I don't suggest that we've polished away all those weaknesses (far from it), but I could see a definite progression. That was good news, right? Well, yes, but the bad news was that trying to beat a meandering four-year-old essay into shape didn't seem to be a good use of my time, nor did it seem to be the best representation of the writers in the Rabbit Room community. It would have been like trying to con-vince people that Lionel Richie was still cool—a mission that's simply not worth the effort no matter how profound "Say You, Say Me" seemed back in the '80s. The writers on our masthead were in vastly different places from where they had been in the beginning—which was the point of the Rabbit Room all along. By locking arms and working in community, we had hoped to sharpen one another. It seemed to be working. Why take a step backward?

So we scrapped that first attempt at a Rabbit Room annual. But like the decla-mation of a prophet, Jonathan Rogers's words nettled me.

When the time came to try again, we decided to stop looking backward. We didn't want a collection of greatest hits. Had there really been any hits in the first place? I mean, does anyone want to get Jason Gray talking about Halloween again? Or read about Andrew Peterson musing on the intersections of Harry Potter and the Gospel? If you define a "hit" by its comment count, those were certainly our biggest singles. So instead of rehashing something old, we decided to furrow new ground. It was time to start "creating culture" as Jonathan might prophesy.

Now let me stop right here and assure you that none of us have the highfalutin idea that the book in your hand constitutes "culture"—well, maybe Jonathan does, but he tends toward hyperbole when he's dressed in sackcloth and standing on his box. Creating "culture" has, to me, the smack of pretense. I think it's safe to say that none of the writers included in this book (not even Jonathan) write for the sake of altering the landscape of our society. However, I think we all hold a funda-mental belief that good writing and good stories can alter the inner landscape of a reader. And those readers, in turn, will go on to constitute the culture we inhabit tomorrow. The distinction here may be pencil-thin, but it is, I think, important. A story, essay, poem, or illustration intent on "creating culture" is easily swept into a torrent of pretense. But a piece of work intent on honoring its reader (or viewer, or listener) is built on a surer foundation of care, love, and responsibility. So are we "creating culture?" That's not for us to decide. You, our readers, will bear out that answer. We are in the business of "creating"; whatever impact our creation has on the culture is a matter best left in the hands of each one of you.

So what is *The Molehill* exactly? Our initial idea was to settle on a theme and send out assignments. After all, a journal needs to feel cohesive, doesn't it? And writers are notoriously fearful of being given *carte blanche*, most preferring a specific topic or theme to write on. But all our attempts to hammer out a theme produced little more than a list of specious titles like "Creativity and the Creative Soul: Mapping the Artist's Inner Journey." Okay, maybe they weren't that bad, but trust me, they weren't much better. So in the end, we threw the map out the window and forged ahead blindly. So be it. Let's see what's out there.

I gave each of the Rabbit Room writers a loose, non-binding assignment based on what I perceived to be his or her strengths, and they took it from there. I even invited Hutchmoot alums Walter Wangerin, Jr., Sally Lloyd-Jones, Don Chaffer, and Justin Gerard to submit work, and to my great delight they agreed. While waiting for those pieces to come in, though, I wrung my hands and worried. How on earth would I be able to put together anything coherent from such a varied cast of characters? I foresaw the coming of a glorious train wreck, and I was tied to the tracks.

Then the work started coming in. Walt Wangerin's was first, and right away, he raised the bar. It was a ghost story. I read it immediately. I loved it. And then I wondered what I'd gotten myself into. Could we live up to the precedent his story had set? But then the rest started rolling in: a short story from Lanier Ivester—an elegant blend of O'Connor and Berry, yet wholly her own; a couple of amazing poems by Don Chaffer; a fascinating memoir from Matt Conner that was born out of tears, grief, and renewal; a trifecta of meditations by Sally Lloyd-Jones from her forthcoming book; a series of hand-drawn recipes from Evie Coates; the good stuff just kept coming.

As the raw work came in and I started editing, unexpected shapes began to take form: parallel lines of thought, echoes, complementary ideas, over-arching themes. To my great surprise, an unlooked-for cohesion emerged. While many readers will most likely skip around as they read favorite writers or head straight for topics that interest them, the adventurous reader who begins on page one and proceeds diligently toward the end will, I think, be rewarded by the shape and flow of the journal as its themes arise and interact with one another. So set your mind at ease; what you hold in your hands is no mere collection of regurgitated Rabbit Room posts. While there are a couple of entries that have appeared in other forms, those have been greatly revised, expanded, and refined. Overwhelmingly, the works you'll find in these pages are fresh and unpublished—*All-Singing, All-Talking, All-Dancing.*

If you stand back and look at it, I suppose you could see this collection as a family photo. It's a snapshot of a group of people and where they are at this moment in time, in their writing, in their lives, in their spiritual journeys, in their understanding of stories and songs and the world around them. This book is, you might say, an Ebenezer stone erected in the wilderness to mark the passage of a common people. It's not an end point; it's a signpost marking the ways we've gone. Whether those ways are right or wrong, good or bad, fine art or rough draft—we invite you to make those judgments on your own.

N. T. Wright was here in Nashville not long ago and he told us that working for the Kingdom is something like being a stonemason. The architect gives us instructions, saying: make this stone in this particular way, and don't ask why. And in faith we go about it. We grind and cut and measure with no idea what the purpose of the stone might be. And when we're done, the architect sees the work and knows its proper use. He tells the strongman on the scaffold to hoist it up, and he tells the man with the mortar and trowel to fit it into place and secure it. And in the end we've all done our little parts and there's a great cathedral that stands tall and blesses the land around it. Out of small efforts, the Architect builds great works. So here we are, an assembly of friends trying to hear the Architect's voice. We haven't set out to create a masterpiece. We're just following instructions. Tolkien's Niggle painted a leaf that became a tree. God knows what may become of this Molehill.

A. S. Peterson
Editor, *The Molehill*

 *vol. 1*

A Prayer from the Bench
at the Bend in the Trail
by Andrew Peterson

I bought this bench for twenty-five dollars.
I searched the papers and called the seller,
Drove to her house, and offered her twenty.
She was stubborn and wouldn't budge a cent.
I drove home with one less fast food combo
In my future and a bench in my truck.

My wife helped me carry it to the woods,
Along the trail I cut through junipers,
Thorns, and clover, where slabs of native stone
Rise, green with fungus from the leafy earth,
Like petrified sea turtles or sperm whales,
Or statues buried a thousand years ago.

We placed the bench at the bend in the trail
Where there is little to see but the trees
And the brown footworn path curving from view,
Disappearing to the left and the right.

Straight ahead is a young hackberry tree
With two knots facing me, narrow windows

In a castle turret where snails stand guard.
There are days when my children come to
The forest, and I can hear in the trees
The magical sound of faerie laughter.
They round the bend, brandishing sticks, march past,
And vanish. I watch with joy and envy.

Now, I have gone through all this trouble, Lord,
To sit, and to watch, and to listen here
At the bend in the trail, on this old bench.
Your humble servant has but one request:
Would you please cast into outer darkness,
For all eternity, these mosquitoes?

Your servant will return when this is done.

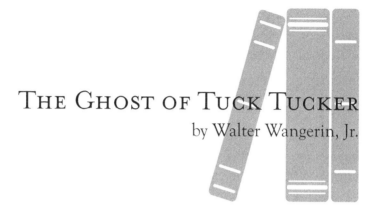

THE GHOST OF TUCK TUCKER

by Walter Wangerin, Jr.

Hammers and tongs
Shall measure this song.

CHAPTER ONE

This here's a story what's got some history behind it.

In seventeen and seventy-six, the year after Dan'l Boone blazed a trail through the tangly woods of old Kaintuck, was a fella named Lamech led seven other big-boned boys—plus brides and babies, you know. Led them mule-packing to west. Did a little trappin', did a little huntin' on the way, fed theirselves on roots and berries, till finally they hit on a patch of good ground. 'Twas a furlong back from a ridge that went an easy slope down to the river.

Mid-spring it was, when the boys commenced to clear some acreage. Felled oak and sycamore. Let's see: chestnut too, beech, yellow poplar. Split the timber, squared it—beams and boards as walls and floors for the cabins. Shakes for the roof. Oh, they put their shoulders into the work, they did. Burned stumps to char, 'n dug 'em out. Dragged chimney stones out o' the fields. Carried weirs to the river for catfish.

Lamech-an'-them was first to break soil for seed, and first to sweep a sickle for the harvest. Had a smith among them, a fiddler, a brewer. Sang hearty. Sang praise to the Lord. Kept the Sabbath. Read the Good Book.

———

I am sitting at the end of the dock where I usually fish. But there's no fishing this summer, because the river has sunk so low that it's cracked clay under my feet. Instead of a rod I bring a book and read.

The year is nineteen thirty-five. I'm twelve. The man who's telling me this story, he is old, old.

Since March not a drop of rain has fallen. The farmers plowed early this year, pulling behind them soft, tall columns of dust. The crops sprouted, but then withered in the fields.

And now comes this old man. I felt him standing at my back. Suddenly he squats and grabs my bare arm, and his hand rucks up the skin on account of his palms are rugged with warts, warts as hard as studs on a belt.

I know the man, but never did talk with him before, nor he with me. No one exchanges words with this old man who lives like a hermit—lives in a one-room stone cabin up river. Moss covers the stone in fur. Folks speculate about how he survives, but it's only that. Speculation.

Now that the old man squats so close by me, I can see that his eyelids are raw and red. But it's with eyes as bright as dimes that he stares straight into my soul. And he scares me. I don't want to be here, but his skinny hand is an iron clamp.

"Y'got the look," is what he says. "I seen you sittin' here," he says, "and I plumbed you, boy. Y'got the piety of mind and the purity of spirit and the glory's own goodness to bear the burden of a man's uncommon sin."

Then he started to tell this story.

Chapter Two

The next year and the next one after that *(the old man says to me),* both the one and the t'other, lost the pluck o' that first year when Lamech-an'-them b'lieved it wasn't nothin' could hold them back. Every least little deed was a victory, and thanks be to God for that.

But they was two weathery winters passed in a row, and some o' the pretty babies took sick and perished, and the frozen earth was too hard to dig a grave, and the sacks of meal run out, and the root cellars emptied—all before folks could turn the earth for gardens again.

Yet and still, almighty God did see them through, and the third harvest and the fourth improved.

They built a church.

They built a school.

The women found jack-in-his-pulpit and re-planted him. They bordered little yards with daisies and rhododendrons and laurel and magnolia and such—and roses, don't let me forget the roses—all o' them just for the beauty. Men whittled bones to toys. They sawed and planed hard maple, jointed it, and fashioned the necessary furniture. So the people woke one morning, callin' themselves a village after all.

And soon it was that other folks come passin' through Kaintuck and on acrost the river to mark out a settlement of their own. Could cross that river best in August when a ford rose up south o' the village a crooked two mile or three. Then a mule could walk the shallow water, and no need to swim.

Now, Lamech-an'-them was a neighborly sort: fed the folk before they crossed on over, fed 'em all their own first year through, and why not? Good to have company, good to have friends for barterin' and for sharin' and for singin' hymns of a Sunday evening.

Well, boy, and time to tell you this next thing, for this here's the true beginning o' the history of Lamech's village:

One day in the greening spring come a fella floatin' a raft south on our north-runnin' river. Had him a mule—a purely white mule—that was ploddin' along the shoreline, pullin' that raft by rope and a bridle against the current, and the shiny-faced fella polin' the bank to keep his raft a ways offshore.

That raft was heaped high with provisions and tools and so.

And didn't the fella hop to dry ground directly below Lamech's village? Did indeed. An' next thing was: he had that mule draggin' his raft up and fully away from the river, out onto a grassy strip of level land. Here, boy, look. See that strip? Yep, 'twas right there.

Soon, then, day was dyin' into chilly evening. Stranger scratched hisself a fire. Stirred a pot o' barley soup. Ate it with a spoon. Washed pot and spoon and bowl in the river. Laid his black, broad-brimmed hat on his black coat—a coat of the cut we call "Prince Albert," too long for the heat, too citified for the place.

By dusk the fella was fast asleep, fearless under the stars, and smilin' clean as a polished fiddle.

"See that strip? Yep, 'twas right there."

Where the old man points his warty finger is at his own stone cabin, solid walls, but the shake-roof sagging sadly downward.

I'm thinking to myself: Must be a true story, if this old man can identify an actual river and an actual place on it.

But then I'm thinking: Well, if it's true, how does he know such details of the stranger?—what he cooked, how he slept. Someone must've been watching the "shiny-faced" fellow, watching close and for a good long while.

The old man has let go my arm, his palm leaving dents in my skin like cleats. And he's looking out over the drought-shrunk river now. But I stick here on account of I want to know more.

I am latched by curiosity.

CHAPTER THREE

W asn't but three days and that citified fella looked to be droppin' a root. Caused the Christians a thin degree of discomfort. No blame on them, though, because the stranger never did show hisself in the village, neither t'market nor to church. Never declared a name. Never so much as offered "Hello."

What I mean: the morning after this oddment made his landing, Lamech-an'- them saluted him from the ridge. Fella looked up and lifted his hat in return. Most polite. And Lamech, lookin' down, said, "God be with you, friend," and the fella kept on smilin', to be sure, but shook his head. Neither did he bid folk to come greet him.

Lamech asked, Did he want some help? Not to impose, (neighborly was Lamech, but respectful of another man's will and of his privacy)—not to impose, said Lamech, but could the village come down with trestle tables and food, and feast the stranger's visitation?

The people was spread along the ridge, left and right of Lamech. And not one that didn't wave and nod agreement with Lamech. Yes, was their meanin', they surely *would* like to break a welcoming loaf with this smilin' sojourner. (Tell the truth, they were hopin' to learn that he was a sojourner and not a settler—especially if 'twould be no river to divide them properly.)

Well, he heard Lamech, and no mistake. Fella turned round and reached behind a barrel and pulled out a turkey plucked naked an' ready for roastin'. More than *he* needed. Coulda match meat for Lamech's bread. But he put his hands together like prayin' and aimed them up to the villagers and bowed, and then what? Well, then he went about his work, and that was that—whilst the Christians stood blinkin' and frowin' down upon the fella's busy back.

But Lamech, he took no umbrage. And he taught the people not to take umbrage. On the following Sabbath he preached near an hour and a half, sayin', "Righteousness requireth kindness." Sayin' with fervor, "And kindness requireth patience!" And the people of God answered him with a reverent "Ay-men."

'Twas but an hour past noon when they got home.

Another hour later—when Lamech had rode his roan mare over-river to preach t' the settlement there—a farmer named Aram gathered the men of the village to lay out a plan of his own. Aram's wife did likewise among the women, sayin', "No force to it, sisters. 'Twill but honor the dapper little man, what we do. Can't be but goodness in giving him gifts."

So each family brought a little something with them to the western ridge: a plowshare, mortar and pestle, needles and a steely sharp awl, tough sinew-thread and tanned deer-hide, and socks, and a honin' stone—that sort o' thing. Then folk processed down the slope, Miss Beulah singin' comfort and welcome on the way, singin' sweet as coral bells:

"I got peace like a river,
I got peace like a river,
I got peace like a river in-a my soul."

She went on and ended with a most convincing voice and verse: "I got love like an ocean," and so.

Must've been Miss Beulah's singing pulled the stranger out'n the woods.

When he saw the village standin' kindly round his raft, and saw gifts at their feet, first thing he did, he put on his Prince Albert coat and that broad-brimmed hat, and smiled and nodded, mute as a stump.

Aram stepped forward and stuck out his hand to shake the stranger's, sayin', "Welcome, welcome, welcome to you, sir."

Right away the stranger doffed the hat he'd just put on, and laid it brim-flat against his breast, and bowed deep, like an Englishman's bow.

So Aram bowed too, then straightened up. "Glad you come by us," he said. "And in proof of our gladness and our welcome," he said, "we come with gifts to see you through the season."

Up close, the people could take this fella's measure: a smallish frame; long, dark, womanly lashes; a smooth chin; a slender, swallowin' neck; respectful eyes, but pupils that did not reveal the soul.

Now, old man Cooper—he wadn't spendin' much attention on the black-coated outsider. Rather, he was squinting at an ax-bit big's the head of a full-growed ox.

Cooper says, "Well, sir, that's a mighty big fellin' ax you got there."

Short fella nods a friendly agreement, so to say: *Big.*

"*Mighty* big, as I was observin'," says Cooper. "Longer handled an' twice as heavy 'n any broadax I ever seen." John Cooper purses his lips and looks directly into the stranger's eye. Then, blunt as a mule, says, "What's it for?"

Aram takes a quick step between Cooper and the quiet fella. "Never mind us," he says. "We're a rough-hewn folk—"

But Cooper interrupts. Says, "Don't speak for me, Aram." And to the stranger, "What? Man asks a question and you don't see fit to talk?"

Still smilin', peaceful as Beulah's river and easy as a drink of water, the stranger answers, "For choppin' trees to logs."

"Well, well, well, lord Cock-o'-the-walk!" hoots John Cooper, puffing his chest for finally crackin' that English walnut's mouth right open: "*Logs,* is it?"

The stranger nods, full of sunshine and refinement.

"So," says Cooper, "what's a frock coat want with timber?"

Old John Cooper, belly-big and hammer-strong, stands there talkin' as if he nor other men been choppin' trees with ax-bits nigh five years now.

But this was a *big* ax, is what I'm sayin'. Cooper hisself could scarce heave the thing to his shoulder and swing it straight.

"My coat's quite satisfied," says the smallish fella, beaming like it's a good joke between civilized men. Then he pokes out his hand, and no help for it but that Cooper must answer with his own, and they shake like the friends John Cooper doesn't want to be, and after a while that gruff man is seen to be kneading his right hand with the knuckles of his left.

The old tale-teller who sits beside me at the end of the dock now falls silent.

Slyly, I run my eyes over him, his furious head, those hands whose palms are full of rivets, and his bare-naked ankles, both of them veiny and pocked with filth. The man's bones are like breakable sticks. His eyebrows are bushels of straw. His skin is as dry as the clay beneath our feet is dry and cracked and flaking.

He does not see me looking at him. With a fierce and glittering eye, my tale-teller is staring at something rusted and half-hidden in the muck-bed ten yards off the dock. The rim of something metal. That's clear. But that is all that's clear, because I can't figure what it is. The anchor of a river barge?

CHAPTER FOUR

Word came to Lamech sayin' that the stranger could talk, did talk, *had* talked with John Cooper.

What? The spiteful John *Cooper?*

Yep, Lamech was told. Cooper went and stood right in front of the man, askin' weasely questions.

Lamech sighed. He knew that their guest rightly deserved a proper apology.

So Lamech walked on down by hisself. He took out his pipe, offered tobacco to the dapper little man who said nay, lit the pipe, drew long, blew short, then uttered the proper, "I am sorry, friend, for the ill treatment we have visited upon you. Wasn't no reason then, an' ain't no excuse now. I am sorry."

That evening whilst he was pacin' among the cabins—for this is how Lamech could best consider matters, by pacin' alone in the dark—he heard John Cooper's growlin' tones. Heard the words, "That struttin' Cock o' the Walk!"—talkin' about the man just granted forgiveness to Lamech for the mouth of *this* man.

Lamech doesn't knock. He pulls the latch an' strides on into Cooper's cabin, an' peers at him for a solid minute.

"You will," says Lamech, "call that good man Tuck Tucker. Hear me, John? Call him by his name. *Honor* him by his name! Humble yourself by use of his name."

And out goes Lamech without another word.

Next Sabbath 'twas Cooper in particular took clear notice of the fact that no "Tuck *Tucker*" came to sit on no church bench. Worse than that: right during Lamech's sermon, Cooper heard that Godless ax *a-chunk-chunkin'* away in the woods. And John Cooper wasn't the only one enkindled by this sinner.

"And look here at this thing now," said Cooper, sittin', he and some men, on his slack-built porch, and smokin' pipes. "Mister, Sir, His Honor, Tucker is buildin' hisself a cabin!"

"Outa them logs?" smith Thompson asks.

"No," Cooper growls. "Out of stone."

"*Stone?*"

"Big river stones."

The mason says, "He ain't asked me to help. You?"

The smith opens his mouth on a great cloud of smoke, then says, "If it's stone, don't seem like the little fella's goin' anywhere soon."

"Nope."

"See what I mean?" Cooper spits his words: "A man don't ask help with heavy labor, and a man don't even come *chat* in a friendly manner, well, I call that man suspicious."

"Uncommon," mutters the brewer.

"A needful man asks, and a kindly man answers"

"Maybe he don't think us kindly."

"Roughed out a trough for mixin' mortar, I suppose?"

"Slick as Saul, *I* say."

And the women? Well, in them days the women hardly could comfort the fears o' their children—or their own fears, truth be told.

All night long: *Chunk-chunkin'!* And over and over the thunder-pops, and the angry screamin' of timber tearin' from its stump, and the rush of branches whipping branches, and finally the *Whump!* of a handsome tree hittin' earth. And all the four weeks of July the forest shook and the tall trunks shrieked, July and two weeks into August, too.

Babies cried. Children crawled bug-eyed and blind in the dark. Families huddled close as rabbits.

A man might say, "Don't know *how* that-ere bantam can swing so big 'n ax."

Miss Beulah might say (and no explainin' how she come to know it), "Tuck Tucker, he wears white sleeves and braces whilst he's wrastlin' logs. And he don't sweat!"

And someone might back her up: "Loppin' limbs, sweatless as a lizard. Like a serpent, seems to me."

"Not one whisker on his shiny cheek."

Chunk-chunk!

"Owly-eyed! Tell me, tell me, what animal is it sees at midnight?"

Villagers' nerves jangled ever' time a new tree toppled: *Whump!*

So here's a mama scolt her children for no reason but nerves. And here's a man hammerin' his thumbs black. Red rashes makin' welts on their babies' faces. And what? A punishing summer. Baneful days. Demon days, a man might say.

Lamech watched the sorrows of his people, how they weighed them down, and he hisself felt sorriest of all. And what can a grievin' preacher preach truer than his grief?

He watched their fears, how the fears was breaking their spirits. And he went and sat with them, and he prayed over their babies, and he begged them, begged them to know that it wadn't nuther God nor nuther the Devil pullin' their souls apart.

But when he went off by hisself, and bended down, and sought in his soul some foundation stone of confidence, it wasn't there. What the people was, *he* was, for that was the sort o' love that Lamech felt for them. Who did wrong? And who did right? Things was comin' to a dire confusion.

CHAPTER FIVE

Mid-August, and Tuck Tucker was choppin' the big limbs off the timber he'd felled all summer. He sawed the tops and the bottoms of their long trunks flat, then he snaked them outta the woods behind his mule. On his strip of land along the river he lopped the branches an' piled 'em up—busy, busy, smilin', and ever' minute keepin' his counsel to hisself.

Of the piled branches Tuck Tucker built roaring night-fires. Close to the river it wadn't no chance they'd touch off a forest fire or ever lick the village. But high-dancin' and howlin' flames can savage the tender mind.

And then the well-dressed little fella was runnin' his logs one by one into the river, where he boomed them round with a long, thick hemp rope.

Lamech thought to hisself, if he couldn't do one thing, he must do the t'other.

So he took his pipe of an evening, and strolled down the slope, and sat in front of the stone cabin on a log carved into a curious bench, an' crossed his legs, an' waited.

Soon came Tuck Tucker back to the cabin for flint and tow. When he saw Lamech sittin' there, he stopped and tipped his head, askin' a question without the word.

"You don't mind?" said Lamech. "I mean to stay a bit. Talk a bit."

Tucker beamed.

He went in the cabin and come back out right finely dressed in his long black coat. In each of his hands was a silver cup, and in the man's pocket, a bottle of rum. He poured two cups and offered one to Lamech.

What took possession of the preacher that evening he didn't know the name of. Not at the start of it, anyways. Maybe he knew it by midnight, but didn't want to *say* the name.

Or maybe Lamech's "Yes" to Tuck Tucker's offer wadn't no more than a yen to be neighborly. A turn-about, maybe, on Tucker's refusing Lamech's tobacco. *Here,* Lamech mighta been expressin' it, *Here's how neighborliness is done.* Out-mannerin' Tuck's good manners, you might say.

14

Lamech sat with the dapper Tuck, the most mannerly Tucker, and talked a little, and drank a little rum.

After a respectful silence, he aimed his pipe stem at them logs was crammed and looped together, and floatin' like some kinda island.

"What then, Tuck Tucker?" Lamech said. "Gon' to build a bridge to ease our crossings over, is it?"

Nope. Nope, it wadn't that.

Lamech nodded and puffed.

"So," he said, stretchin' his long legs and leanin' back, a man in blessed company. "So: You lookin' to build a deep-bellied flat boat, so's to ferry goods to and fro the villages? And up an' down the river?"

Nope. Tuck Tucker never did consider such a plan. Not a boat, not a transport.

As dusk sank into darkness, Lamech numbered down the possible uses for Tucker's logs. And no, and no, none of those.

A pallisade wall to keep out heathens?

Bigger barns? A granary?

The two men turned their talk into a kind of swapping game. This thing? Not that thing. How about that thing? Not this thing, and so, and so.

When Lamech awoke the next morning, he was sick with internal afflictions an' suffered a brain stretched tighter 'n a drumskin. Folks was standing outside his cabin, murmurin' together.

He stepped out and said, "What?" for he was ignorant both of their meanin' and of their mood.

Straightway they told him what—the very what that Lamech hisself had revealed to them in the small hours before the dawn. When he finally remembered the whole of it, Lamech was sore troubled in his heart, and he wept.

'Twas a gleeful John Cooper sat close to front in the church when the congregation gathered at noonday. Oh, a chipper John Cooper, might even say *triumphant* John Cooper, for he was right and Lamech was wrong, and on top of that, Lamech was sour with drink!

Aram, on t'other hand, was down to business and merciful.

First things first: Whatever can the village do now?

For Tucker told Lamech a story of gold and glamor!

Said he meant to build *mansions* of his logs. Mansions in a golden city down south and south to the shores o' the *sea*. Gonna ride his logs on up this river, then down another river that flowed wide as Kaintuck itself. For far "below," said Tucker, is a Beulah-land where men don't bury bodies underground, and walkin' on those fields was like walkin' on a carpet of sponge and water, where folks talked in a Frenchified tongue. Tuck Tucker, goin' to take *their* forest to the golden streets, the golden streets. . . .

Well, Lamech spoke to the congregation, sayin' he knew no mansions except those the Lord done promised his Christians. *In my father's house are many mansions!* The word of the Lord! And *I go to prepare a place for you.* For us. For Christians! But Tuck Tucker, he wadn't no Christian, so far as Lamech could make him out. So, what sort of mansions could Tucker be talkin' about? The Lord's is up. But the black-coated man was going *down* an' *south!*

Who could parse the meanin' of that?

And what is a people to do now?

'Twas Miss Beulah herself stood up and quoted scripture as clean as could Lamech. *"And the great dragon was cast out,"* she sang in a hymn-singin' voice. *"The great dragon, that old serpent, called the Devil, and Satan, which deceiveth the whole world!"* She said, "Revelations twelve and first nine," then sat herself down again.

Well, then Lamech saw it as his own duty—he, the leader of his village and the foremost of sinners—to go down the slope and try one more time to speak Jesus to Tuck Tucker before that man could put his plans into action. For Lamech would not have the sly fella takin' the dreams and the soul of his people off and away with him.

———

Suddenly my ancient story-teller, he jumps up, vibrating like a fiddle-string and pointing at that rusty out-crop of metal.

"Can you shift it?" he cries to me. "Go on over there, an' tug at that blade, an' see if you can't lug it to surface again."

Something inside me cannot refuse the old man's command. I hop down from the dock. I crunch dry clay underfoot until my bare feet sink in the thick, moisty muck surrounding the object of the old man's desiring.

I squat and take hold of the rim of the metal, and pull and pull, and can shift it only a little. It frustrates me no end. I hunker close, and dig with my hands, and throw up handfuls of muck, then lean my shoulder against the steely thing and move it a little more.

"It come visible," the old man shrieks, "in the river-drought. Never did see it again till now, but there it is. There it is! Pull it, boy. Rock it! Pry it out!"

CHAPTER SIX

At the pop of sunrise the village folk ran over to the ridge and, *hooo!* how they laughed in such happy relief, on account of the logs was still floatin' there, boomed on the river, not gone anywhere, and not one of them lost.

But when they dashed with their jiggling joy on down the slope, the strong-backs first, the light-boned behind them, things took a different turn.

Tuck Tucker's head was chopped clean off his body. And smears o' blood on his ax told how it was his head come off. And was a long flush o' blood was cuttin' channels to the river, and a trailing stretch of river water blushed.

No signs of a struggle, no. Nothin' but that broad-brimmed hat laying neat on Tucker's folded coat—neither no sorrow among the villagers. For 'twas a good and necessary deed been done here, an' praise God that the Devil had his due.

Women did not wash the dead man's corpse. Men bound it to his monstrous ax, and rowed out a ways, and dropped the whole mess overboard and gone, so good and gone.

Lamech put a name to the ceremony. Said, "He goeth whence he cannot come back again—into the night, into the land of shadow where even the light is as dark as death."

Of a sudden Miss Beulah threw wide her arms and sang:

"And the smilin' devil
That deceived them
Was cast in the brimstone lake,
The lake of fire for Jesus' sake!"

"And that," Miss Beulah shouted in a fit o' joy, "is also in the Book of Revelations, and Ay-men to everyone now. Ay-men, ay-men to all."

CHAPTER SEVEN

As it did do—an' would do all down to this blameful year—the river slumped and that ford three mile south of the village rose up again. Folk could cross horseback again.

So two men of Lamech's village rode south and crossed over at noon o' the day, spent the afternoon tradin' barley meal for maple syrup, then, 'long about twilight, started ridin' south to cross back over again. Half a mile south, an' one fella whispered to t'other, "Samuel, look-it there."

Samuel, he looked like—you know how it can be—looked like lookin' through a fog, and saw what his friend was seein'. Was a third man—hisself but a shadow, but mounted on a sheet-pale beast—that was ridin' the far bank south, and matchin' the village fellas step for step and canter for canter.

They kicked their horses to a gallop. The instant their heels hit flank that shadow-man's beast was gallopin' too.

Samuel grinned. "Nate!" he yelled. "It's a race!"

So they leaned low to the necks o' their horses, narrowed their eyes, hissed breath through their teeth, and concentrated on speed.

T'other man kept perfect pace, bolt-erect no matter the slap o' the wind.

Coursing, flat coursing the moonlight to the three-mile mark, all three riders pulled up at the ford at the smack same time. A tie! And Samuel an' Nate set their horses splashin' over to greet that fella that could ride as swift as them. Met him in the middle, and lost their laughin' in fear.

For the shadow-man, well, he had no head. And sat a mule silvery white under a moon both full and round.

Man said to them, courtly and quiet, "Show me your hands."

Well, wasn't no choice to it, but to extend their hands and open their palms.

The headless man stayed stark still a minute or two, then said, "No," and turned his mule and cantered upriver to deep water and disappeared.

Bug-eyed and panicky, Samuel and Nate crossed over and high-tailed it home, and found them some liquor and drank, and drinkin' loosed their tongues, and they told their ghost story to anybody would listen.

Now then, village folk kept judgment to theirselves. For their neighbors was drunk, after all.

Wasn't but three days later, and John Cooper hisself come gallopin' home, clear-headed an' telling the same story, an' village people commenced to feel the same fears as them that brought fear back with them.

Lamech was silent, meditating.

Aram said, "You eat something yet? Come on inside. It's time you et."

Trials an' afflictions, fears and opinions—the village huddled and wondered, an' wasn't no end to it all.

So then, Lamech stuffed his black Bible in a saddle bag and mounted his own horse. First, he walked it to Tuck Tucker's stone house. 'Twas hollow. Not a stick of furniture in it, nor food nor drink. Hollow.

He turned to south and rode at a slow walk.

He looked over-river. His guts started to squirm discomfortably. For he too was unblest, for he too saw the dark man astride his foggy-white mule, ridin' the far bank step for step with Lamech's walkin' horse.

'Twas long and long, the three-mile course, but Lamech added no speed to his goin', an' kept holding high his dim lantern that showed him nothing but his own flickerin' self. Unlike the men before him, he *knew* he was approachin' a haint. And his purpose—terrible in itself—was to strive for some sorta peace for the sake of his people.

Under the waning moon it was his ear, not his eye, that recognized the ford at his horse's hoofs. He started in to crossing.

So did the haint on his ghost-mule.

They met in the middle. Lamech rustled his Bible out an' clasped it one hand whilst he lifted his lantern in t'other. But the flame reduced itself to a blue bud on its wick. He tried to quote scripture: *Blessed is the man that walketh not in the counsel of the ungodly.* . . . But his tongue stuck like paste to the roof of his mouth.

Suddenly, shadows dashed the waters. Shadows reached out an' seized the lantern. The flame flared up like a house afire, but it felt cold and moist on Lamech's face. What he saw, he saw a small body dressed in a neatened coat an' nothing between his shoulders.

A dignified voice said, "Lamech, show me your hands."

Lamech sat fixed. Could not move.

The haint had substance. He reached out, took hold on Lamech's wrists, twisted them till the palms was upmost, and there even Lamech could see a score and more of hickory splinters in the skin, suddenly stinging Lamech like a score of needles.

With womanish fingers the black-coated haint started pluckin' out the splinters. One by one, tiny jets of blood came shootin' from the wounds.

"Oh, Lamech, Lamech," said the voice. And then it said, "Wash in the river."

Straightway the muscled mule reared up, and leaped into the air, and mounted night, and the ghost of Tuck Tucker was never seen again.

Lamech washed. The stings cooled. But when he pulled his wet hands from the river, every little blood-fountain was a wart.

⌇⌇⌇

I cannot shift the metal more than an inch in its socket of muck.

My ancient story-teller bumps me aside. He takes a firm grip on the rusted edge and, in spite of his gaunt face and skinny arm, heaves the whole thing up, and lo: it is an axhead, impossible huge.

Thin blood streams from his palms. The blood becomes a writing on the ax. The writing says, "Lamech, Lamech."

The old man stands up, sunken to his knees in the muck, and cries out, "I have confessed my sin in innocent ears! My God, I have confessed mine iniquities!"

From his red-rimmed eyes now falls a flow of tears, and I am set free.

The anvil's still ringing
For faith and good breeding.

"Wise is the man who sets his contemplation upon the mole; wiser still is the man who seeks the hill and climbs it."
—Benjamin Franklin, Father of the Electric Kite (WNI)

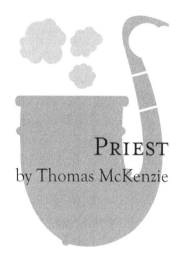

Priest
by Thomas McKenzie

Man was created priest of the world, the one who offers the world to God in a sacrifice of love and praise and who, through the eternal eucharist, bestows the divine love upon the world.
—Alexander Schmemann, *For the Life of the World*, Chapter 5, Section 4

You have made them to be a kingdom and priests to serve our God,
and they will reign on the earth.

—Revelation 5:10 (TNIV)

Priests are different.

I mean that in a number of ways. For one thing, they are different as in "strange." My wife Laura and I used to ask ourselves the following question: Do strange people become priests, or does being a priest make a person strange? The answer seems to be "yes." The priests I know have extreme personalities. If they are quiet, they are very quiet. If they are angry, they are very angry. If they are kind, they are very kind. There isn't much middle ground. They are opinionated, often about a wide range of subjects. Many are socially awkward. Often they are inscrutable. Yes, I'm oversimplifying and being judgmental. Which goes to my point: we priests are different.

For one thing, adults don't often dress in uniforms. When they do, they get noticed. When people see a police officer, most prepare to follow an order. When people see an adult in a McDonald's uniform, they prepare to place an order. When people see a soldier, they may prepare to express thanks. But when people see a priest, most look the other way. I don't know of a uniform that enlists more turning aside than that of a black shirt and a white clerical collar.

I was ordained more than a dozen years ago. On the day I was ordained, after the service, I had to fly from Pennsylvania to Texas. I decided to wear my new priestly uniform. I wondered how it would feel. I wondered if people would ask for prayer. I wondered if people would be unkind to me, or especially friendly, or if they would be deferential. I wondered if I would be enlisted to give counsel or to explain the ways of God. But that wasn't what happened.

A little girl stared at me; her mother took her hand and told her to stop. The man who took my ticket called me "Father." No one else even spoke to me. I sat on the second row of a completely full Southwest flight—an airline on which you get to choose your own seat—and passenger after passenger checked me out, then moved past, toward the back of the plane. The last person to board chose to cram herself between two especially large people rather than sit at the end of my otherwise empty aisle. How did I feel? I felt different.

I am different. People who know me know that I'm a bit strange. I was strange when I started this work. I may be more strange now. I wear different clothing. My daily schedule is different; I don't even have a normal weekend. The books I read, the things I think about, the conversations I have are all pretty unusual. My taxes are so different that I have to use a special kind of accountant, one that only works with my kind of people.

The Latin root of different is *differre*, from *dis* ("away from") and *ferre* ("carry"). It means "to set apart." I am carried away. I am set apart. According to the 39 Articles of Religion, a key statement of Anglican theology, all priests have to be called, chosen, and sent (Article 23). The Church goes through a rigorous process of summoning, preparing, and releasing her priests. We are poked and prodded. We are trained and educated. We take vows. We make promises. This means that the sinners who wear collars are supposed to be different from the sinners who don't. And believe me when I tell you that many lay people care about that difference far more than I do. Some of them deeply value that difference, and not always for healthy reasons.

On Sunday mornings I put on different clothes. I wear a white robe that is meant to hide my individuality and remind us of the purity of heaven. I wear a rope for a belt that is meant to remind me of my slavery to Christ. I wear a stole (a kind of scarf) that both indicates my priestly authority and recalls in me the yoke of Jesus. I wear a chasuble (a kind of poncho) to remind me that I'm a citizen of a different Kingdom.

When I worship with my sisters and brothers, I am called upon to do three things that they are not. I bless the people. I pronounce forgiveness on the repentant. I hold the bread and cup in my hands and say: "This is my body . . . this is my blood." I do these things because in those moments, in that community, before that table, I am in the place of Christ. I do what Christ alone would do were he physically apparent to us. I bless, I forgive, I celebrate—because that is what he would do, because that is what he does. Some say that the priest is "the icon of Christ."

All of this different*ness* can do things to a person. It can humble you, break you, inspire you to prayer and repentance. *Jesus Christ, Son of God, have mercy on me, a sinner.* It can also drive you to relish your difference, to believe you are better than, higher than, greater than. Alexander Schmemann said: "If someday 'pastoral pathology' is taught in the seminaries, its first discovery might be that some 'clerical vocations' (calls to the priesthood) are in fact rooted in a morbid desire for that 'supernatural respect.'" This sense of difference can lead to self-justification and the committing of horrible sins. If people feel they are different, they may believe the normal rules of moral behavior do not apply to them, and they may sometimes feel above (or beyond) the law. I am deeply troubled when I hear of fellow priests using their difference as a license to harm God's children and bring shame on the Body of Christ. This is despicable behavior. Inexcusable.

These abuses have led some to ask: "Why should we even have priests?" Some branches of the Church get along quite nicely without them. After all, Christianity is "not a religion but a relationship." Priests are vestiges of the old ways, of pagan temples and sacrificial rites. Priests are go-betweens, intermediaries between God and Man. In most languages, they are called the "offerers of sacrifice." They stand at the bloody altar and call on Heaven and Earth to meet. That is what they have always been set apart to do, whether Roman or Mayan or Jew. "What does any of that have to do with us?" some might ask. "What does a priest have to do with our modern religion? We don't need priests," the enlightened modern Christian might say.

Rather, some Christians seem to need "speakers" to encourage and inform, CEOs to lead, and rock stars to sing praises. We Christians do everything in our power to make the Church like the rest of the world. We don't want difference, we want sameness. One pastor recently said: "We would do anything to be relevant to the culture." Anything to be relevant. What is relevance but sameness? When a church says they are 'relevant," what do they mean but that "we dress like you, look like you, talk like you, think like you?" After all, St. Paul said, "I have become all things to all people so that by all possible means I might save some" (1 Cor. 9:22 TNIV). Sameness is the road to salvation, or so we are told.

St. Paul also said, "God gave me the priestly duty of proclaiming the gospel of God, so that the Gentiles might become an offering acceptable to God, sanctified by the Holy Spirit" (Rom. 15:16 TNIV). That does not sound like a man who is trying to be like everyone else. That sounds like an old-world priest, standing between God and Man, offering the Gentiles themselves as his sacrifice.

Then we have St. Peter reminding us that "you also, like living stones, are being built into a spiritual house to be a holy priesthood, offering spiritual sacrifices acceptable to God through Jesus Christ" (1 Pet. 2:5 TNIV). *That* is the New Testament priesthood. *That* is the sacrifice. But who is the priest?

Maybe the priest language bothers you. Maybe you think it's egotistical for me to stand in the place of Christ and be called by the old word. Fair enough. But the thing that should baffle you and bother you is not that I am a priest. The thing that should baffle you and bother you is that *you* are also a priest.

I was not made a priest because I'm different. I was made a priest to remind you that you are different. I am a poor example that calls forth this greater reality in you. The blood of Christ was shed for you; this saves you from your sin, certainly, and praise

God for that. But that blood does something else, something related to forgiveness; that blood makes you a priest and says that you will reign on the earth (Rev. 5:10).

The first priest wasn't some pagan witch-doctor dancing around a fire. The first priest was Adam in the Garden. Humanity stood at the center and pinnacle of creation, set there to reign over the earth. Adam was given the power to name, and therefore rule, all of creation. Humanity was set apart, made different from all other creatures of God. Male and female they were made in the image of God, unlike any other thing. Our First Parents were made different to be God's partner in the ordering of all things—but they failed.

After their failure, many priests arose in their place. Many men and women, of many languages and religions, sought to bring order to chaos, to make the right sacrifice that would align Heaven and Earth—they failed.

God himself sent us the Law, with its orders of priests and sacrifices and its Temple. The priests were there to bleed the sacrifices, to save us from our sins, to put right what had gone wrong. But "it is impossible for the blood of bulls and goats to take away sins" (Heb. 10:4 TNIV). Where priests failed, the Messiah has succeeded. The Book of Hebrews tells the story of the Gospel from this perspective: that Jesus has become our great High Priest and has offered the great sacrifice, once and for all, in his body on the cross.

The work of the Cross is over and done; the great sacrifice has been achieved. But if the sacrifice is complete, in what way are we priests? Certainly not as bleeders of animals. The writer of Hebrews says it this way, "Now may the God of peace, who through the blood of the eternal covenant brought back from the dead our Lord Jesus, that great Shepherd of the sheep, equip you with everything good for doing his will, and may he work in us what is pleasing to him, through Jesus Christ, to whom be glory for ever and ever. Amen" (Heb. 13:20–21 TNIV). In this world, we are given this priestly task, the work of the eternal covenant, of allowing God to "work in us what is pleasing to him." We live in the inaugurated Kingdom, but we still pray for the Kingdom to come. So now we stand again at the center of creation, fallen but redeemed. Now we stand again in God's garden, weeds growing but lovely nonetheless. Now we stand as priests in the

Name of the present-yet-absent Christ because that is our calling, our joy, and our responsibility.

As priests, I suggest that we have three primary tasks. They happen to be the same responsibilities I have each Sunday morning in our Anglican worship service. Firstly, we are called to bless both God and others. Sometimes blessing is a verbal act, as in saying the words: "May God bless you." But there's much more. We bless as we participate again in the Genesis project, by bringing order out of chaos. When the Christian assembles ideas and words into story, she is working as a priest. When he gardens to the glory of God, he is living as a priest. When you write a song, or build a house, or raise your children in the Name of Jesus, you are serving as a priest. We bless when we intercede for others, when we bring them before our Lord in prayer and supplication, as he constantly does for us. We bless when we love, especially when we love the unlovable. Most of all, we are called to bless God by giving him the honor and praise that is due his Holy Name.

Secondly, we are called to forgive. "If you forgive the sins of anyone, their sins are forgiven; if you do not forgive them, they are not forgiven" (Jn. 20:23 TNIV). Now that we have been forgiven, how do we dare not forgive another's sin? Forgiveness is what we need, and by "we," I mean all of us, in the Church and in the world. When we release sin, we release suffering. When we forgive, we acknowledge that all sins, even the ones that we are most ashamed of and the ones that have hurt us most of all, have been paid for by our High Priest. The final priestly sacrifice has been made. Our job is to proclaim: "It is finished."

Third, we are called to celebrate the feast of Communion (1 Cor. 5:8). Jesus said, "I am the living bread that came down from heaven. Whoever eats of this bread will live forever. This bread is my flesh, which I will give for the life of the world" (Jn. 6:51 TNIV). As priests we stand at the intersection of Heaven and Earth. That intersection is the Body of Christ. This was true of Jesus's literal, physical self; and it is true of his Body, the Church; and it is true of his Body in Holy Communion. We are called to worship the One in Heaven while bringing his life to the ones on earth. He is the bread; we are the eaters and distributors of that bread. We are like the disciples at the feeding of the five thousand, taking food from the hands of

Jesus and passing it on to others. We do that through participation in the life of his Body, the Church. We do that by celebrating this strange means of grace, the Holy Communion. We do that by sharing the goodness of Christ with the spiritually and economically poor. His body gives us life while also sending us on a mission to those who are starving for him.

Imagine now that you are what God says you are: a priest. You are not just a consumer of religious ideas and Christian entertainment. You are the one called apart, carried away, set aside. You are "a chosen people, a royal priesthood, a holy nation, God's special possession, that you may declare the praises of him who called you out of darkness into his wonderful light" (1 Pet. 2:9 TNIV). This means that you are blessed, loved, needed, and accepted. It means that your life has purpose and value and meaning. It means that you are more than you realize. And, yes, it means that you are different—maybe even strange.

We are an odd people with strange priorities. Our sins are numerous. But the grace we've received is total. We make many mistakes. We are sometimes ignored on airplanes, or in churches, or at family events. Our difference sometimes comes with a cost. But we are also thankful to be different, for in our difference we have been given a precious gift. We have a ministry to the whole world, a ministry of light and life, of blessing, of forgiveness, and of celebration.

Yes, we priests are different.

"AMAZING! ASTONISHING! YOU NEVER READ ANYTHING LIKE IT! Ladies and gentermen, folks of your obvious discernment, intelligence, and beauty can't afford not to own a copy—no, multiple copies—of *The Molehill*. So unpocket them coppers. Form a line! No pushing, please!"
—PROFESSOR FLOYD WENDELLSON, Feechie Lecturer, Phrenologist, Purveyor of Fine Medicinals, Literary Expert (WNI)

THE FLINTKNAPPER
by Jonathan Rogers

It was ten o'clock and hot already. Six of us leaned against the trucks parked under the big pecan tree in front of the shop, some smoking, some sipping tepid coffee from styrofoam cups, some staring absently. It had been a slow morning at Cargill Plumbing Company. By the time the first smoke break rolled around, two of the crews hadn't even left yet, and DeWitt and Jenkins were already back after unstopping a toilet at a fraternity house. The lone entry in the morning's job log, recorded in DeWitt's crabbed hand, simply read, "Idiot tried to flush turkey leg."

How many mornings had the men of Cargill Plumbing Company gathered beneath this very tree? Here the older plumbers freely offered their wisdom to the younger—tricks of the plumbing trade, advice about women, old anecdotes worn shiny with use, teaching lessons of dubious morality.

The young plumbers, in return, offered up their foolishness. They detailed their adventures in local bars and roadhouses—every fistfight, every flirtation, every game of pool, every ill-advised bet. They planned their next stratagem in the war between plumbers and roofers that has continued time out of mind. Most especially, they told of their hunting and fishing exploits.

These stories of outdoor adventure were one of the important ways by which the unofficial pecking order was established and maintained at Cargill Plumbing

Company. Seniority entered into the equation, of course, as did professional acumen, but mostly it came down to qualities of manliness that find their purest narrative expression in the hunting story, in which a man imposes his will on his surroundings by bold and decisive action.

By these lights, Rusty Hedrick, the lead plumber on Truck 2, was clearly the alpha dog at Cargill Plumbing Company (Mr. Ralph Cargill, the owner and my kinsman, excepted). It wasn't just that Rusty was an avid and proficient hunter. He was a boar hunter, and his methods were very little different from those of, say, Gilgamesh, or Nimrod, that "mighty hunter before the Lord."

Two or three nights a week, Rusty took his dogs to the floodplain swamps beside the Ocmulgee River. He turned the baying hounds loose to track the wild hogs that grew fat and mean in the bottomlands. The catch dogs, wide-headed bulldog mixes, strained against their leashes, but Rusty held them, stewarding their energy for the fight ahead. When the long, throaty howls of the chase changed to higher, quicker yips, Rusty knew the hounds had bayed up, and he and his catch dogs made for the racket in as straight a line as the landscape would allow.

The bay dogs cautiously surrounded the boar without exactly engaging him; the bulldogs barreled right through their perimeter, snarling, snapping, and foaming at the mouth, fearless to the point of foolhardiness. The fights were tremendous. A wild hog could weigh as much as four hundred pounds, and his clacking tusks were often four or five inches long and sharp as knives. When the dogs eventually latched onto either of the hog's ears, often at the cost of considerable injury, Rusty wrestled the whole struggling mass to the ground and tied the boar's flailing hooves with a rope, all the while doing his level best to avoid the tusks thrashing in every direction.

Rusty showed us pictures of the boars he caught—black, hulking, bristling, wild-looking things that looked altogether out of place in the pens where he fattened them until cold weather and killing time. He showed us the bruises where he had been kicked and the scars where he had been slashed. He brought us smoked hams from wild hogs, and sausage and barbecue. One morning he called in sick because an alligator had eaten one of his dogs as it swam across the river in pursuit of a hog—heartsick, he said, and I don't doubt it.

I ate Rusty's barbecue, and I listened to his stories. But I got a bellyful of both long before my coworkers seemed to.

For my part, I had little to add to the stock of hunting and fishing lore that was exchanged beneath the pecan tree. My hobbies run more to the artsy and craftsy, so to speak. I am a flintknapper. Like the Indians of millennia past, I chip flint (or, more properly, chert) into projectile points—arrowheads, as they're commonly known. It's a surprisingly technical process, requiring that the flint-knapper see and understand the many intersecting planes along which the flint is going to break when he strikes it—planes that seem to change with every flake that flies. A controlled shattering, I call it. A good flintknapper has the foresight of a chess player or a political strategist. He looks at the situation in hand and not only sees every angle but knows how to work it. And I am one of the best of the flintknappers.

I won't bore you with the details, but I will say this: a few years ago the Folsom point was considered unreproducible, which is to say, unforgeable. Nobody under-stood how the Great Plains Indians of last Ice Age got such delicate fluting out of flint. Today there are eight or ten people in the world who can make a Folsom point, and I am one of them. In the flintknapping world I'm something of a celebrity, in fact. People collect my points, and I give lectures and demonstrations at the knap-ins that are happening at some state park or rented pasture somewhere in Middle America almost any weekend of the year.

You might be surprised to know how little weight any of that carries with the plumbers at Cargill Plumbing Company. I've quit talking about it to my coworkers unless they ask, and they only ask so they can mock me.

On the Monday morning in question, the plumbers had just finished being amazed at Rusty's account of capturing two hogs on a single outing when DeWitt turned to me and said, "How about your weekend, Ronald? Did you go to one of your swap meets?" The plumbers always referred to my knap-ins as "swap meets," for the mere pleasure of harassing me.

"I did not," I said.

"Well, "DeWitt persisted, "what did you do instead?"

I paused, then stepped over to my truck, opened the door, and pulled out the spear that hung in the gun rack. It was a beautiful weapon, tipped with a Folsom point of reddish chert that I had hafted on a five-foot hickory pole. I gestured toward DeWitt with it. "As a matter of fact, I killed an alligator with this spear."

There was another pause. Creased brows. Cocked heads. Then DeWitt broke into a grin. "Haw haw!" Everybody else laughed too. But I didn't laugh. I gave them a dignified gaze modeled after the expression Rusty put on after describing an especially triumphant boar hunt.

"Do you think I'm joking?" I asked.

"Of course you're joking," Jenkins said.

"Or lying," Charlie suggested.

"You can't kill no alligator with a spear," Jenkins said.

I snorted. "Can't kill an alligator with a spear?" I shook the spear in Jenkins's direction. "Do you realize that during the last Ice Age, Great Plains Paleoindians killed mastodons with weapons exactly like this? *Mastodons!*"

"Naw, naw" Jenkins clarified, "I meant *you* can't kill no alligator with a spear."

"Oh-ho!" I said. "Now I see what this is about. You think a man who went to college can't possibly have killed an alligator with a spear." This was a long-running theme. Some of my plumbing colleagues behaved as if my going to college was a badge of shame. I don't think they understood how bad it really was. I hadn't just gone to college; I had gone to graduate school to study anthropology and dropped out of the Ph.D. program with only the dissertation to go.

Rusty sighed. "Nobody cares if you went to college, Ronald."

"Yeah," Charlie chimed in. "You were young back then. Everybody acts the fool when they're young."

"It wasn't going to college that was foolish," I said. "It was coming back here to work with y'all. I should be tenured by now, you know."

"I know, I know," DeWitt said. "You told us all about it. Departmental politics. Folk science. The blind spots of academic antherpology."

"Blind spots," I said, "Exactly. They think digging up burial sites and reading papers at conferences is going to . . ." But I trailed off. DeWitt's eyes were shining, and I realized he was making sport of me, sending me down a well-worn trail.

Charlie looked at his watch. "You'd better speed this along, Ronald, or you ain't going to get to the Smithsonian rant before break's over."

Jenkins chuckled. "I don't know what you can do with a spear, Ronald, but I believe you could talk a alligator to death in about a minute and a half."

Everybody howled at that. Things were getting pretty festive at my expense; in the middle of the exuberance, Cody, Rusty's helper, snatched the spear away from me and went into what I guess he thought was some kind of Chickasaw war dance, raising the spear with both hands and bending at the waist and pumping his knees almost to his chest and chanting and whooping and generally making a fool of himself.

"Stop it, Cody," I shouted. "That's a lethal weapon you're flailing around." The plumbers had another fit laughing—not at that moron Cody, if you can believe it, but at me.

"A lethal weapon!" Jenkins snorted, and then he went into that wheezing laugh of his.

"You're damn straight it's a lethal weapon," I said. "That's a Folsom point, my friend. Many a buffalo succumbed to a Folsom point hurled by a Great Plains Paleoindian. Mastodons too."

"Yeah, you mentioned the mastodons," Rusty observed, drolly.

Cody came whooping and stomping up behind me. If I had been thinking straight, I would have tackled him around the waist, but instead I went for the spear shaft, which he snatched away as if it were part of his herky-jerky war dance. He gave a little crow-hop and was gone on another loop of the gravel driveway. I resisted the temptation to chase after him; I was scarcely maintaining my dignity as it was, and I didn't figure it would help any to go chasing a boy fifteen years my junior across a gravel parking lot.

"How about alligators?" chimed in Charlie.

"What about alligators?" I asked.

"How many you reckon have succumbed to a Folsom point?"

"Well, I can't say for sure, Charlie." My tone was so superior and detached that not even Charlie could miss the rebuke. "But before yesterday I suspect it had been a good five hundred years since a man had gone down to the Ocmulgee River with a flint-tipped spear made with his own hands and killed an alligator and then skinned it out with a flint knife, also made with his own hands."

By now Cody had quit the war dance and was waving my spear around like a light saber and making Jedi noises.

"You boys seem to think this is some kind of joke," I said, "but the last man to do what I did was probably a Creek Indian, about the time Hernando de Soto came through and gave everybody smallpox."

Cody jobbed the butt-end of the spear into the gravel and leaned against the shaft, panting a little. His brow was creased; he was working hard to think up some new way to make a fool of himself. Rusty gave him a little sideways nod and raised an eyebrow, and the boy shuffled over, shame-faced, and handed the spear back to me.

Rusty does that kind of thing all the time, and it just burns me up. He acts like he's being a friend to you, doing you a good turn, when really he's reminding everybody that he's the alpha dog, able to bring any of us to heel with a stern look.

Charlie and Jenkins pursed their lips and raised their eyebrows at one another like a couple of old dowager aunts, and I waded right into them. "I saw that look," I said. They exchanged another look. "I saw that one too." Everybody was against me.

"I don't understand this," I said. "I tell you about an alligator I've killed—I even show you the spear I killed it with—and you all assume I'm lying about it. But let Rusty come to work and launch into one of his stories about the latest wild boar he's tied up in the woods, and every one of you goes to cooing like a schoolgirl: 'Ooh, Rusty, weren't you scared when you wrestled down that hog?' and 'Ooh, Rusty, how big was the mean old boar you caught this time?' and 'Ooh, it's hunting at its purest—it's man versus beast.'" I was mightily tempted to spit on the ground. "Pure hunting? Are you joking me? Rusty's hunting dogs have radio controlled collars. With GPS tracking. They've got Kevlar flak jackets to protect them from hog tusks—the dogs!"

Rusty shrugged. "I love my dogs."

Everybody murmured their approval of Rusty's humane sentiment.

"Ronald's right," DeWitt said. "We haven't been fair." He turned to me with a sly smile. "Why don't you go on and tell us all about how you killed this alligator of yours."

Perhaps you think this was exactly what I was hoping for—an opportunity to tell a hunting story worthy of Rusty himself while my coworkers gave me their undivided attention. In fact, it was at this point that my confidence began to waver, and I'll tell you why: I hadn't killed any alligator. I wouldn't even know how to begin killing an alligator with a spear, though I once saw a sixteenth-century drawing of six Timucua Indians ranged battering ram-style along a lance they were jamming into the gaping maw of an alligator so big they looked like pygmies in comparison— half a dozen miniature St. Georges slaying the dragon.

It was true enough that I was in possession of a dead alligator. From a quarter mile away I had seen it wander onto Highway 96 from the floodplain swamps of the Ocmulgee River, just in time to get run over by a cream-colored LTD piloted by a woman whose white hair didn't even show above the headrest except when she thump-thumped over the poor thing. No brake lights. No swerving. Just the straight-ahead progress of grim inevitability bearing down. The great scuted tail seized up into the air with the impact of the front tire, then the back tire sent the big alligator rolling—once, then twice, then half again so that it lay in the road with its white belly up to the sky.

I don't make a habit of picking up roadkill, but this was as fresh as it gets. I had often wondered if the flint tools I made were adequate for the skinning of an alligator. So I wrestled the thing into the bed of my truck and took it home.

It never occurred to me to claim I had killed the alligator myself until five seconds before it came out of my mouth. But there it was, and now I was determined to see it through.

"Well," I said, and cleared my throat a couple of times. "I'm sure you know the broad bottomlands this side of the river along 96."

"I know it well," said Rusty. Somebody snickered. DeWitt, I think.

I cleared my throat again.

"You okay?" Charlie asked, reaching out solicitously as if to pat my back.

"Well, I had noticed where an alligator had wallowed out a spot under the power lines..."

"Is that right?" Jenkins asked. "Just strolling by, I reckon, and noticed this alligator?"

This wasn't going well. My colleagues were grinning at me like a pack of monkeys. But I soldiered on. "Anyway, I figured I could hide behind a log with my spear at the ready..."

I was facing the shop, so my back was to the road. I saw that nobody was looking at me any more, and then I heard gravel crunching behind me. The grins left the plumbers' faces, replaced by quizzical looks. I turned around to see a white truck rolling slow up the driveway. On the door was a gray decal in the shape of Georgia and the words "Department of Natural Resources." The mustachioed driver wore the khaki shirt and brown ball cap of a game warden.

I watched the progress of the truck, and Rusty and Jenkins and Cody and Charlie and DeWitt all watched me. There was something new in their eyes. It occurred to them for the first time that perhaps I actually *had* speared an alligator.

Before the truck had rolled to a stop, the warden knew I was his man just by following my coworkers' eyes. The truck door opened and a brown boot crunched on the gravel and then another, and the warden stretched himself to a good 6-2, adjusting his ball cap in a way that would have seemed more appropriate if he had been wearing a wide-brimmed trooper's hat. He was rangy and walked like he had probably been a baseball player in high school.

He looked at me, then at my spear, then at the others, then back at me. "My name's Officer Bennett," he said, "Georgia Department of Natural Resources. I'm looking for a Ronald Weaver." He was looking directly at me.

"I'm Ronald Weaver," I said. "What can I do for you?"

"Mr. Weaver," he said, "would you mind stepping over here to my truck?" He gestured politely, professionally toward the bed of his own truck. I don't know why I did it, but I looked over at Rusty. He nodded as if to say, "You probably should."

I walked over to the warden's truck, and the other plumbers followed close behind. There, spread out so that it covered almost the whole bed of the truck, was an alligator hide. The plumbers elbowed one another and shot me admiring looks. Charlie whistled. "You weren't lying, were you, Ronald?" Officer Bennett pretended not to have heard him. He was a professional first and last.

"Mr. Weaver," the warden said, "do you recognize this alligator hide?" All eyes were on me. I nodded my head, and there was a warm murmur from my coworkers.

The flies had already found the hide, which was pretty gamey in the midmorning sun. They spiraled and hummed over the bed of the truck. "Darby called you, didn't he?" I asked. The warden pretended not to have heard that either. But I knew it was Darby.

Darby was my next-door neighbor. He put up a privacy fence between our yards, which is his prerogative, of course, but what chapped my hide was the fact that he didn't put up any privacy fence along the back edge of his property, nor did he seem too worried about protecting his privacy from the neighbor on the opposite side. He just put up eight panels of wooden fence, apropos of nothing, right there by my knapping shed and rock pile, where I keep my old lawnmowers and the shingles that the landfill wouldn't take, as if he couldn't stand the sight of me a day longer. I've heard that good fences make good neighbors, but there's something mighty unneighborly about a privacy fence, if you ask me.

When I skinned out the alligator, it got dark on me before I finished scraping the hide; a hand-flaked flint scraper turns out not to be the most efficient implement for the job. I needed to spread out the hide until I could get back to it, so I flopped it over Darby's privacy fence, the front end on his side and the tail end on mine. I threw some salt on it hoping to knock down the smell, but the flies were going at a steady hum when I left for work that morning.

With the benefit of hindsight, I will admit that it wasn't the most neighborly thing I've ever done. Nevertheless, it seems to me that if Darby had a problem with it, the manly thing would have been to call me and talk about it. Instead, he called the Department of Natural Resources.

Officer Bennett turned back toward me. "Mr. Weaver, do you know that the alligator is a federally protected species?"

I studied the face of Officer Bennett. How was it, I wondered, that he could be so confident that he was right and I was wrong? The Creek Indians never had to put up with this sort of thing. When they needed an alligator, they went down to the swamp and got one.

"Mr. Weaver," the game warden repeated, "I asked if you understood that the alligator is a protected species."

In his khaki shirt Officer Bennett looked for all the world like one of those park rangers who frog-marched me across the National Mall in front of the Smithsonian Institution. They asked the same kind of obvious yet irrelevant questions. Maybe it was a technique they taught at the school for park rangers and game wardens.

"Do you realize it's a criminal act to assault a director of the Smithsonian Institution?" the ranger in DC had asked. He might have meant it as a rhetorical question; the fact that his knee was between my shoulder blades made it hard for me to give him an answer in any case. But I spit out a couple of pieces of pea gravel and pled my case while they handcuffed me. "First of all, he's not a director. He's Assistant Director for Pre-Columbian Cultures." This while they were hauling me to my feet. "Second, I didn't assault him. I bumped him in the course of a spirited discussion. And third, he started it."

That was true. He did start it. I wish somebody would explain to me why it's a criminal act to bump a man, maybe give him a small shove that knocks him into a display case that should have been bolted down better if they didn't want their ancient pottery getting knocked over and skittering across the floor, but it's not a criminal act to insult a man's intelligence and denigrate his life's work.

I had gone to the Smithsonian offering to teach a faculty workshop on "Problems and Methods in Paleoindian Lithic Manufacture Technologies." I was offering, in other words, to bring the practical insights of a flintknapper to bear on the overly academic anthropology practiced at the Smithsonian and places like it.

I had even brought a sampling of my Folsom points to show that I knew whereof I spoke. The Assistant Director for Precolumbian Cultures looked them over, then gave me a little simper and said my points were quite good "in a folksy kind of way." He said the staff of the Smithsonian were fully qualified to teach their own workshops, thank you very much, but he did offer to buy up to two dozen of my points to sell in the gift shop. I imagined my Folsom points, the work of my hands, languishing between the snow globes and the T-shirts, being pawed by sweaty tourists.

The alleged assault happened about one second after that.

My dissertation director threw me overboard a week later, and a week after that I hired on at Cargill Plumbing Company.

It's a peculiar thing, I don't mind telling you, to leave a world because you don't belong there and to come back to your hometown and find out that you don't belong there either. It makes a fellow feel like a man without a country. But there in the shade of the pecan tree in front of Cargill Plumbing, something had begun to change. Even Rusty looked at me as if I were an initiate in his fraternity, or maybe a comrade-in-arms.

"The penalties for alligator poaching are steep," Officer Bennett continued. "A minimum fine of a thousand dollars and as much as a year in jail for the first offense."

The plumbers gasped as one. I, on the other hand, took the news with admirable calm. My coworkers were impressed, I believe, at the fact that I didn't protest my innocence or otherwise make excuses. I was all sangfroid.

The game warden was still at it. "In addition we will confiscate the vehicle you were driving when you harvested the animal, as well as the gun you shot it with."

A heavy silence fell as I pondered Officer Bennett's words. Finally I spoke up. "Officer, I'm afraid there's been a mistake." Everyone's eyes narrowed.

"I didn't shoot any alligator," I said. Charlie gave a smirk and a little nod as much as to say, *Just as I suspected*. Rusty looked at his feet and sighed, wishing, I think, to spare me the embarrassment of his direct gaze.

I raised my spear, and the morning sun glinted off the polished chert of its point. "Anybody can shoot an alligator," I said. "I speared mine."

The plumbers whooped their unalloyed admiration. I honestly think they would have launched into "For He's a Jolly Good Fellow" and hoisted me onto their shoulders if the game warden hadn't stepped between us.

As Officer Bennett and I rode away, I turned to give the boys a thumbs-up. Since my wrists were cuffed together, I gave them two.

There's Power in the Name

by Ron Block

A child is clothed from birth with many names. Some are good names: Loved, Able, Strong, Intelligent. Others are not so good: Unloved, Victim, Bully, Despised. Regardless of the nature of the names, the essential truth is that they are rooted in the instability of temporal things, like temperaments, talents (or lack of them), and nobility (or ignobility) of birth.

We can carry the name of Straight-A Student or Abused Child from childhood into adulthood, and it will bear fruit, good or bad. But these labels are rooted in the temporal; they are clothing we wear, created by our families, or our school years, or made with our own hands as we sew fig leaves together to "be somebody." Temporal names often hide our real, God-created self, or as George MacDonald puts it: "God's idea of us when he devised us." It's essential to go deeper than the temporal names we carry. This idea of naming begins at the very beginning, and we shall not know ourselves until we know, in the end, our true names. Creation itself holds its breath against the day when the sons of God will be revealed. We must know the nature of Christ living within us and the God-given names we carry.

In Genesis, the Creator repeats a theme. He creates, and then he names what he has created. "Let there be . . ." is followed by "Let them be called. . ." God creates by naming and then further names the thing that has become.

"And God said, Let there be light: and there was light. And God saw the light, that it was good: and God divided the light from the darkness. And God called the light Day, and the darkness he called Night. . . . And God said, Let the waters . . . be gathered together unto one place, and let the dry land appear: and it was so. And God called the dry land Earth; and the gathering together of the waters called he Seas: and God saw that it was good" (Gen. 1:3–5a, 9–10 KJV).

Then we find a change in theme. God makes a man from clay and names him Adam. He brings the animals to Adam for naming; the Creator thinks it important for Adam to take part in naming the world. God tells him also not to eat of the Tree of the Knowledge of Good and Evil, or he will surely die. In other words, God creates the world, creates the man, and names the situation.

Next he creates the woman. One day the serpent finds her and lies to her. "God is holding out on you," it says. "You will be made wise by taking matters into your own hands." She has a clear choice between God's naming and the serpent's words. She chooses wrongly. Suddenly Adam and Eve notice they are naked, and they are ashamed. They create their own coverings, putting leaves together to make clothing to cover their shame. They run from God, rather than running to him for covering.

After the Fall, God mentions the woman having children. Consequently, Adam names her Chavvah, meaning "Life." "And Adam called his wife's name Eve [Chavvah], because she was the mother of all living" (Gen. 3:20 NKJV).

For the first time, animals are killed to cover human nakedness. God himself does this for his beloved humans. They sin, and there are consequences, logical ones. They cannot live forever in this state. But he loves them and names sin's price: blood. He shows them also that he is the one who covers their nakedness.

Eve has a boy, and she names him Cain, meaning "Gotten" or "Acquired," because she had acquired a man, her firstborn, her beloved, from the Lord. She has another son, Abel, meaning "Breath" or "Vapor." His name proves prophetic, as his life would be merely a breath compared to her own.

One day Abel brings a blood sacrifice from the best of his lambs, the covering named by God when he sacrificed animals to cover Man's sin as well as Man's body. Cain brings his own sacrifice, the fruit of the ground. But God accepts Abel's sacrifice and not Cain's. Why? Because Cain wants to name his own price. He wants to be his own boss. He wants to "make a deal with the Man upstairs" on his own terms. He is self-concerned and wants to make sure the deal works out in his favor.

But the universe runs on God's terms, not ours. So Cain is resentful, and God reasons with him patiently. "So the Lord said to Cain, 'Why are you angry? And why has your countenance fallen? If you do well, will you not be accepted? And if you do not do well, sin lies at the door. And its desire *is* for you, but you should rule over it'" (Gen. 4:6–7 NKJV). God has named the terms of sacrifice and the situation. Cain has a choice here: either to get with God's naming or not.

Cain leaves in anger, even though he does end up giving a blood sacrifice after all—the blood of his brother. In his petulance at not being able to name his own price, in his anger that the works of his own hands are not enough for God, he kills his brother Abel, stabbing a life-long dagger of sorrow into the hearts of his parents. He trusts his own naming of the situation, of the necessary sacrifice. In Cain's one-act play of self-fueled unbelief, Adam and Eve lose both sons.

Even afterward, he isn't repentant. He's still looking out for himself, worried about his punishment, worried about what dangers await him, and not at all thinking of Abel, or of his mother and father. Self-concern is the continual fruit of one who refuses to accept God's naming.

Abram and Sarai were promised a son by God. By the time the promise was given, it was already a laughable impossibility. Years pass, and every year, as the barren waste of winter is followed by the fertility and lush fulfillment of spring, Abram and Sarai feel the mocking laughter of flowering trees. Sons and daughters are born to friends, servants, and neighbors. The calendar turns again and again. Sons and daughters are born to other sons and daughters. Children's children run and laugh in the late afternoon fields of harvest, and still nothing.

Eventually, they lose heart. Sarai says: "I've got an idea, Abram. The clock is ticking. We're getting old. Take Hagar, my servant, into the tent and make a baby. Then we're sure to have the promised heir. Maybe God helps those who help themselves."

Ishmael is born. He is the product of the self-effort of Abram and Sarai. God comes to Abram and says, in essence, "No, that's not the way this works. Self-effort doesn't produce the works of God. Sarah will have a son by you. Impossible? Just watch." God changes Abram's name to Abraham, meaning "Father of Many," in preparation for Isaac and the coming nation of Israel.

At last, Isaac is born and grows up. God has promised that Abraham's descendants will come through him, but Isaac isn't married, has no children. One day God tells Abraham, "Take Isaac, take your only son, and offer him." But Abraham knows God will keep his word. Descendants have been promised through Isaac. If Isaac dies, God will have to raise him from the dead. Abraham puts his full trust in God's naming. The heart steels; the hand tenses on the handle of the sharpened blade; the arm raises to plunge deep into the skin, muscle, and heart of that long-awaited and cherished son. And God says: "Stay thine hand."

—⁓—

Isaac's wife, Rebekah, is pregnant with twins. They are struggling in her belly, so she goes to the Lord. The Lord names the situation for her: "Two nations *are* in your womb, two peoples shall be separated from your body; *One* people shall be stronger than the other, and the older shall serve the younger" (Gen. 25:23 NKJV). In other words, the birthright will be given to the youngest. God names the situation, but no one is paying much attention.

Esau, son of Isaac, son of Abraham. When he was born, they named him "Hairy." Even from birth, he is a man's man. Esau becomes mighty, a man of the field and a cunning hunter, confident and self-assured. He's got it made. Dad loves your venison, Esau.

Jacob, second son. He was always second place, born grasping at the heel of his firstborn twin. They named him "Heel Catcher" or "Supplanter." He grows up a homebody—plain, ordinary, a mama's boy, living among the tents.

But God doesn't see the outer appearance of things. He looks at the heart.

Esau strides in one day after hunting, and he's famished. He smells the red lentil soup Jacob has made. Mama's Boy is cooking in the kitchen, and the Mighty Hunter is hungry. Jacob believes in his given name and schemes for the birthright. Heel Catcher says, "Sell me your birthright, and you can have some." Esau, self-confident, self-assured, thinks it's a game. He dishonors the promise God made to Abraham. "I'm about to die of hunger. What good would this birthright do me then? Fine, have it. I swear it over to you. Give me the soup." Esau trusts in his own ability to name his life, to name his own situation, and he spits a bowl of red lentil soup in the shining face of the promise of God.

Later, Jacob takes advantage of his father's blindness, pretends to be Esau, catches at the heel once more, and takes the blessing that would have been his brother's. Esau swears to kill him, and Jacob runs away. O, ye of little faith. "The older shall serve the younger," thus saith the Lord.

Time passes. Years go by. Jacob runs into his swindler of an uncle, Laban, Rebekah's brother. Cheats run in the family, and God knows Jacob needs to feel what it's like to be cheated. Fourteen years go by. Leah, Rachel, children come along.

After all that striving to gain and grasp the birthright blessing God had already promised him, Jacob heads back to the promised land. But Esau is coming to meet him with four hundred men—Esau who had been cheated, who had sworn to kill his twin brother. Jacob sends gifts.

There in the night, by the ford of the river Jabbok, Jacob wrestles with a peculiar Man. Finally seeing that the source of all blessing is God, he will not let the heavenly messenger go. The Man gives Jacob a permanent limp, a symbol of weakness, and still Jacob will not let go. "I will not let you go unless you bless me!" cries Jacob. The Man says, "What is your name?" In essence, *Who do you think you are?* And the son of Isaac says, "Heel Catcher." That's the name he has believed in; he has accepted the knowledge that the "heel-catching" manner of his birth and his history of trickery and deceit will define his character forever. But Heel Catcher is not his true name, the name held for him by God.

The Man renames him. "Your name shall no longer be called Heel Catcher, for you have struggled with God and with men, and have prevailed." Jacob's new name is "Prince with God," or "Israel." It is an entirely new identity. "You will no longer be called by your old identity, but by the new one." A nation is born.

───※───

Hundreds of years later, the growing nation of Israel cries out for a flesh-and-blood king, just as years before, wandering in the wilderness, they said, "We are sick of eating this stupid bread from heaven every day. We want meat." They rejected the sustaining provision of God, their daily bread, for something they could turn into quail jerky, something that would last longer, something that would relieve them from having to worry about the next day. Now they wanted a king. It was the same old story. "This God, providing for us daily, protecting us, this invisible king, we don't want that. We want someone we can see. We don't want his naming. We want to name our own lives.

God says, "Okay. But this king is going to take your sons to be in the army, to work his lands, to make weapons and chariots. He'll take your daughters to be bakers and cooks. And he'll take your fields, and vineyards, and olive groves—the best of them—and give them to his servants. He'll tax you, taking a tenth of your harvest of seed, and he'll give it to his officers and servants. A tenth of your sheep will be his, and you will be his servants. You're going to cry out in pain because of the king you have chosen, and I am going to let you taste the consequences." But like Adam and Eve, like Cain, like Abraham at times, and like Isaac, Rebekah, Jacob, and Esau—they don't listen.

Samuel goes to Saul, son of Kish, of the tribe of Benjamin. Saul says, "What? King of Israel? Why me? I'm from the tribe of Benjamin, the smallest tribe. And my family in that tribe is the least of all the families." But Saul is big, and strong, and tall. He looks kingly. In fact, "Desired" is his name.

But Saul is a king only in physical appearance. He quickly proves to be selfish, power-mad, and unjust, an insecure man who refuses to trust God, who tries to name his own terms, who wants to run his own life and do things his own way. He makes excuses for everything. He does what he wants and then thinks God should bless it.

David is an artistic boy, a dreamer shepherding in the fields of his father. He's a thinker as well, fed on Israel's history of mighty men of faith like Moses, and of great battle commanders like Joshua, and of the successes and failures of judges like Samson. When emergencies come, as they inevitably do, David is a courageous doer. A bear comes to kill sheep. David looks at the bear. It's a heck of a lot bigger than he is. David feels the adrenaline of fear pump through his heart and limbs, but he looks to God. God is far stronger and far bigger than any bear. David's name means "Beloved." As the beloved of God, he shores up his courage, steps out in faith, and kills the bear. The same thing happens with a lion. These are just practice sessions for his face-off with Goliath, in which God's power, manifested in one man who trusts in his name, would be on display for all Israel.

When Goliath comes along, every man in Israel is afraid, including Saul. Goliath shouts, "I defy the armies of Israel this day; give me a man, that we may fight together" (1 Sam. 17:10 NKJV). David, a shepherd boy with no armor, is outraged at the insult to the God of Israel. "For who *is* this uncircumcised Philistine, that he should defy the armies of the living God?" (1 Sam. 17:26b NKJV). David outshines the entire army of Israel in courage, and he delivers a great speech to Goliath: "You come to me with a sword, with a spear, and with a javelin. But I come to you in the name of the Lord of hosts, the God of the armies of Israel, whom you have defied. This day the Lord will deliver you into my hand, and I will strike you and take your head from you. And this day I will give the carcasses of the camp of the Philistines to the birds of the air and the wild beasts of the earth, that all the earth may know that there is a God in Israel. Then all this assembly shall know that the Lord does not save with sword and spear; for the battle is the Lord's, and He will give you into our hands" (1 Sam 17:45–47 NKJV). David names the situation by faith through knowing God and his naming.

As the giant Philistine arises in anger at this seemingly empty boast, this seemingly mindless insult, David runs toward him, reaching for a stone in his leather bag, fitting it into the cloth of the sling, swinging, swinging, and then releasing the stone in faith. God honors David, because David honors God. The stone crushes through the skull bone of a giant forehead.

David's life for the most part is one of trust in God's naming. God has named him "Beloved" and "King." Because of the favor upon him, the favor of both God and man, David is persecuted by Saul. Those who trust God will be persecuted by those who do not. Saul fears him, and this king of unbelief hates the king of faith, as Esau despised his brother Jacob and his own birthright, as the Pharisees hated Jesus. Saul repeatedly tries to kill David. And in time, David has opportunities to kill Saul as well. When Saul lies sleeping and David stands over him, spear in hand, the thoughts come. *One thrust of the spear and it's all over, David. Just one impulsive, quick motion. You won't have to run anymore. You'll be king of Israel.*

David's men couldn't understand why he ignored such opportunities. But David trusted God's naming of him as king, realizing that it is God who would have to bring it to pass. Samuel had anointed Saul king by God's direction. And David refused to gainsay God's anointing. God had spoken, had named the present king, named the future king, and David knew there was no need to help God out by exerting effort of his own like Abraham and Sarah had with Hagar.

Though David has his moments of extreme failure, as when stealing Uriah's wife and murdering him, David has a core of faith rooted in God's power and love. The gross sins he sometimes commits reinforce for him the nature of God's forgiveness and mercy, because at the heart of this "man after God's own heart" is faith in the God of love and hope and promise. The God who names also loves David, whose name is "Beloved," and David knows that God's assessment of all people and all situations at all times is one hundred percent correct.

We often talk about Jesus as though things were easy for him. We think of him more as God than as man, if we really think of him as a man at all. In reality, by coming to live on earth, the eternal being set aside the use of his omnipotence ("I can of Myself do nothing" (Jn. 5:30 NKJV)), the use of his omniscience ("But concerning that day and hour no one knows, not even the angels of heaven, nor the Son" (Mat. 24:36 ESV), and "Who touched me?" (Lk. 8:45 NKJV)), and his omnipresence. He became a single soul localized in a single body in a single regional area. All use of his divine attributes was set aside, and Jesus became a man who had to be completely dependent upon the power and direction of the Holy Spirit. "I can do nothing of myself," he said. "I do only as I see the Father doing." Though he remained God, the second person of the Trinity, he operated wholly as a man dependent upon the Father. "I do nothing of Myself; but as My Father taught Me, I speak these things" (Jn. 8:28b NKJV).

Jesus hears God's naming of him. He is Jesus, the new Joshua. His name means "Jehovah is salvation." Born of a virgin, he's the promised Messiah, who will save his people from their sins. He's the true king of Israel. His mother spoke the naming of God over him, held those things in her heart for her son, and he read the Scriptures, seeing himself as in a mirror. Prophecies of location and circumstance were fulfilled at his birth, and when he was two years of age, the mothers of Bethlehem wept for their toddlers as prophesied by Jeremiah. Jesus was being named with the strongest naming in all of history: Messiah, Savior, Prince of Peace, Redeemer. He took those names into himself as his identity, in faith, confounding teachers in the temple at twelve years of age.

When Jesus was thirty, God spoke to him from Heaven. "You are my beloved Son, in whom I am well pleased." Beloved Son. Pleasure of God. God has spoken.

Conversely, the Pharisees and Sadducees were always trying to name themselves by their doings. "God, I thank You that I am not like other men—extortioners, unjust, adulterers, or even as this tax collector. I fast twice a week; I give tithes of all that I possess" (Lk. 18:11–12 NKJV). Comparison and competition were the names of their religious games. John the Baptist calls them a generation of vipers. Jesus ends up calling them all sorts of names such as vipers from Hell, whitewashed tombs—and a very telling one: children of the devil. They were of the same mind as Cain, which really went back to the serpent. These were men who wanted to name themselves, name their own sacrifices, and name their own righteousness by their own human effort, by the works of their hands, by their human lineage.

John 8 dramatically depicts these two worlds in conflict. The woman taken in the act of adultery is dragged before Jesus and flung to the ground. "Let him who is without sin among you be the first to throw a stone at her" (Jn. 8:7 ESV). They drop their rocks. "Neither do I condemn you" (Jn. 8:11 ESV). A conversation follows between Jesus and the Pharisees where they repeatedly attack his identity; they insinuate an illicit birth and suggest that he doesn't know who his father is. They attack his divine naming. They say, "Where is your Father?" and then, "*We* were not born of fornication" (Jn. 8:19, 41 NKJV). *Like you, bastard.* They also ask, "Who are You?" (Jn. 8:25 NKJV). *Who do you think you are with all this confidence in God, with all this assurance of who you are? Your Father bears witness of you? You are not of this world? If we don't believe you, we'll die in our sins? You have heard from God? You do always the things which please him? Who do you think you are?*

When Jesus says, "Before Abraham was born, I am," taking on the name of God himself, equating himself with the voice of the burning bush, the debate is over with a bang. They go into fits of rage at his blasphemy, and suddenly they are picking up their rocks again. But it is not yet his hour, and Jesus the Savior, Messiah, and King of Israel walks through their midst and leaves the scene.

It is no accident that his next action is to make a blind man see. He uses his spit. The Pharisees are so consumed with their own independent self-effort that the divine words from his mouth seem blasphemous. *Are words from God's heart not good enough for you? Here's what even my spit can do. Also, you miss the point that you are just clay, and you need God in you to be fully human.* Then Jesus mixes his spit with clay, as God breathed into the clay of Adam, and gives sight to the blind.

In Gethsemane he wrestles on his face in agony, sweating, weeping. He looks ahead at the coming days and sees not only execution, but worse: separation from his Father. He sees himself becoming sin, enduring the divine disapproval, though all his life, eternal and earthly, has been bathed in divine love and acceptance. The filth and muck of a lost humanity held hostage by "the prince of the power of the air, the spirit who now works in the sons of disobedience" (Eph. 2:2, NKJV), was about to be put inside him. But he knows his God-given names: Savior, Redeemer, King. He also knows his less pleasant names, just as true: Scapegoat, Passover Lamb, Intercessor, the Man who Stands in the Gap. In the end, the answer given him is final: Silence. "The cup which my Father has given me, shall I not drink it?" He is a man who lives from the divine naming.

—⁂—

When Jesus died, all who have put their faith in him throughout human history were put in him. Note the past tenses in this passage from Ephesians: "And you He made alive, who were dead in trespasses and sins, in which you once walked according to the course of this world, according to the prince of the power of the air, the spirit who now works in the sons of disobedience, among whom also we all once conducted ourselves in the lusts of our flesh, fulfilling the desires of the flesh and of the mind, and were by nature children of wrath, just as the others. But God, who is rich in mercy, because of His great love with which He loved us, even when we were dead in trespasses, made us alive together with Christ (by grace you have been saved), and raised us up together, and made us sit together in the heavenly places in Christ Jesus, that in the ages to come He might show the exceeding riches of His grace in His kindness toward us in Christ Jesus. For by grace you have been saved through faith, and that not of yourselves; it is the gift of God, not of works, lest anyone should boast. For we are His workmanship, created in Christ Jesus for good works, which God prepared beforehand that we should walk in them" (Eph. 2:1–10 NKJV).

In Christ, we died to that Ephesians 2:2 spirit and were resurrected as new men. "Therefore if any man *be* in Christ, *he is* a new creature: old things are passed away; behold, all things are become new" (2 Cor. 5:17 KJV). That old spirit of death, of selfishness, has been replaced with love for God and others. We have been named eternally with a new name. Paul said in Ephesians 3:14–15 (NKJV), "For this reason

I bow my knees to the Father of our Lord Jesus Christ, from whom the whole family in heaven and earth is named . . ." This new nature is not merely new outer clothing; it is an essential change of name, of source, of nature.

Why do so many of us go so long without living in our new identity? Why do we spend years exerting all our effort on a hamster wheel that leads to nowhere?

One problem is that we believe in the old names. We often trust the voices of our childhood, of our sins, of abuse, of the devil, of our accomplishments or the lack of them, more than we trust God's voice. We name ourselves by the sins we have committed rather than leaning into our new names. We so often say, "I am a sinner saved by grace," when in reality we have been given a new nature, a new Spirit. We believe in a sinner identity and think we have to strive by our own effort to overcome it. That negative faith bears negative fruit: sin. We get stuck in Romans 7, doing things we hate and not doing the good we desire because we are trusting in the false-reality of the old creation rather than in the true-reality of the new. We often hate our humanity and sew fig leaves of false identities to cover our shame.

Another trouble is that many of us don't even know our new names. We are ignorant of our true name, our true nature, in a world that has been chicken-scratching for its immortality for centuries, and we don't even know it for ourselves. We are named with the Father's nature, the Holy Spirit—Holy, Beloved Saints, Vessels of Mercy, Children of a Heavenly Father. But we have not sufficiently searched the Word to find these facts, much less appropriate them and live from them daily.

The third dilemma is that even when we know our new names, we may not be relying on the source of the names. Cognitively, we know that we are saints—accepted, beloved, holy—and yet we have gained no inner revelation of that intrinsic reality, no real conception of an immanent and indwelling Christ. We do not take our new nature by faith, and as a result, the new nature does not take us over.

Why do we have this disconnection? What wakes us up to our identity?

Abraham had to learn to see the impossibility of conception by Sarah. He had to accept his inability to make God's promises come to pass by human effort. He had to come to terms with his broken nature. By the time Isaac is to be sacrificed, we see an old man who immediately trusts God and obeys.

Jacob had to struggle to gain blessing through Laban, that swindling uncle. He had to be wrestled to the ground by the messenger of God—an angel or, as some believe, a pre-incarnate appearance of Jesus Christ. He had to have his hip thrown out of joint, leaving him to walk with a limp. He had to see that all his striving resulted only in brokenness, weakness, and the realization that God is the only power.

David learned his lessons early. He saw the bear, then looked at himself and saw weakness and inability. He looked at God and saw power, and he made the connection of faith. That lesson bore fruit in the severed head of a gigantic, mocking Philistine; it bore fruit for his whole life (with a few exceptions).

Jesus knew his innate human weakness. "I can of Myself do nothing" (Jn. 5:30 NKJV). The perfect man was perfectly weak, and so with true strength was perfectly strong. He let himself be named with the naming of his Father, though the world, the flesh, and the devil himself came against him.

Power is perfected in weakness. Jesus had to learn obedience by the things he suffered. Hebrews 5:7–10 (NKJV) says of Jesus that "in the days of His flesh, when He had offered up prayers and supplications, with vehement cries and tears to Him who was able to save Him from death, and was heard because of His godly fear, though He was a Son, *yet* He learned obedience by the things which He suffered. And having been perfected, He became the author of eternal salvation to all who obey Him, called by God as High Priest 'according to the order of Melchizedek.'" It is a shocking idea that the Son of God had to learn something. But he did. He set aside the use of his omniscience to become like us; for our sakes he had to go through what it meant to learn things progressively, to trust the Father's names for him when everything around him screamed the contrary.

When I was in my teens and twenties, I lifted weights. The bar is lifted from the bench, and its weight presses down on the arms. The arms lower the weight down then push it back up. Doing this repeatedly tells the arms, "Hey, build more muscle." In the same way, we are schooled in faith on the bench. We learn obedience by the things we suffer. In all of us there is a heavy weight of names set against faith in God's naming. We have the gravity of the names of childhood—The Abused Child or The Shamed Boy or The Victim—or even positive ones—The Good Brother or The Smart One. We often lay for years on the bench press, under the heavy weight, without realizing it can be lifted and even thrown off. Years go by, the weight of the old identity begins to crush us, and we cry out to God. Like Saul, we have gone on our own steam, sought our own way. Eventually, like Saul surrounded by the Philistines, we want to fall on our own swords. We despair, like Paul in Romans 7, of ever being what we are meant to be.

But that is precisely the time when Paul cried out, "O wretched man that I am! Who will deliver me from this body of death? I thank God—through Jesus Christ our Lord!" (Rom. 7:24–25a NKJV). The blackest time is the best time for God to show his love and power, and we often don't see our need of God's naming until things are dark, until the old names have run their course. This is especially true of "good" names. It is harder for those rich in money, fame, good looks, talent, a good temperament, or other assets because those things can be a placebo. "Brass is mistaken for gold more easily than clay is," said C. S. Lewis in *The Great Divorce*. We can mistake an identity based on our gifts, our performance, and the approval of others for our true God-named identity. But earthly riches don't last. In the end, we will go out as naked as we came, with only Jesus Christ as our covering. I will not go out as Ron the Musician. I will go out as Ron the Christ-follower, the Christ-relier, the Christ-truster. Wood, hay, and stubble will burn away to reveal whatever gold, silver, or precious stones remain.

Surrounded by the enemy, beset by mortal danger, David would cry out to God. Goliath, Saul, Absalom—David escaped nearly every trap set for him, because he was God's Beloved King, a name given him not by men, but by God. He let God define him. We can escape every trap as well if we lean into God's naming of us, if we lean into the gift of being "partakers of the divine nature" (2 Pet. 1:4, KJV).

If God's view of things is not fully correct, he isn't much of a god. If his naming of his people, of their situations, isn't fully correct, he is not worth trusting. That's always the issue. It started in Eden with the serpent. If I can distill it down to a quick idea, it's this:

1. God creates and names reality. He names us, names the situation. God told Adam, "In the day you eat of it you will surely die."

2. Our perception of circumstances contradicts his naming. The serpent came along and said, "You shall not surely die," and extolled the virtues of going against God's naming.

3. We choose. Eve's inner choice wavered between God's naming and the serpent's lies. When the switch was thrown to the serpent's side, darkness followed instead of light.

4. Our action is the result of the inner choice of what, or who, we choose to trust. Eating the fruit wasn't the choice; it was the outcome of a choice already made. "I believe the serpent." Action follows inner choice.

5. Consequence follows—whether negative or positive.

And God said, "Let there be Abraham, Father of Many." And God said, "Let there be Israel, Prince with God." And God said, "Let there be David, Beloved King." And God said, "Let there be Jesus, God with you." And God says, "Let there be you."

How have the world, the flesh, and the devil named you? We live breathing the mental atmosphere of a world which runs counter to God's thoughts, to God's ways. The world is steeped in a performance-based mentality: attain godhood by self-improvement, by self-actualization. The names given by the world, the flesh, and the devil can be negative or positive; no matter, as long as they don't keep you from knowing your real names, the names given by God. Like Eve, like Cain, like Saul, and like David, our sins, as believers in Christ, spring from an inner choice to disbelieve God's naming, even if we don't realize we're making the choice. *We don't want this stupid manna. We don't want this invisible King. We don't want this eternal naming. We want some meat. We want a real, visible king. We want to name ourselves. I want someone else's talent. I wish I had his house. If only I'd had a better childhood.*

God's naming doesn't come from what you have done, what the world calls you, what your fears tell you, what the devil says. It comes from the eternal God; it is the result of what Jesus Christ has accomplished. Beloved. Accepted. Holy. Saint. Set Apart. Redeemed. Washed. Cleansed. Complete. Filled Full in Christ. Partaker of the Divine Nature. Dead to Sin. Dead to the Self-Effort Promptings of the Law. Alive. Whole. New Creation in Christ. Seated in Christ at the Right Hand of the Father. Son or Daughter of God. Indwelt by the Spirit.

Christ is the source of all our new names, and he gives them freely. And our minds say, "But . . . but . . . but . . . but . . ." *But, I'm a sinner. But, yes, we are all those things, positionally—but not actually. But I was hurt as a child. But my dad didn't love me. But I can't get victory over A, or B, or C. But I should at least be trying to be more like Jesus. But I've got to keep the Ten Commandments. But I am a failure. But I am a success.*

But nothing. Yes, we have hurts. Yes, we have doubts. Yes, we have fears. We are human. Jesus had them; he grew up in a poor community and was viewed as a bastard child. But in Christ we are partakers of the divine nature. We're not independent, self-actualizing beings climbing a mountain by self-effort to attain godlike status. We are instead dependent vessels of the Holy Spirit, given everything we need for life and godliness right here, right now. If we depend, rely, trust, abide, will Jesus Christ not come through for us? Is he not able to cause our stones of faith to hit dead center in the foreheads of our Goliaths? Will not the Philistine army be routed? Does he not live within us, Christ in us, the hope of glory?

Will we trust his naming? Or will we continue to live from old names? We have a choice, really the only choice offered us: the decision to trust God as the source— or not. In Christ we are new creations, named with a new name, filled full in Christ. "I am the resurrection and the life" (Jn. 11:25 NKJV). Do *you* believe this? That's the relevant question.

"One does not read *The Molehill* in order to believe in hills. One reads *The Molehill* in order to believe that moles exist inside them."

—G. K. CHESTERTON (WNI)

God's Little Finger
by Sally Lloyd-Jones

King David was marveling at God's universe.

"When I look at your heavens, the work of your fingers, the moon and the stars, which you have set in place, what is man that you are mindful of him...?"
—Psalm 8:3–4 (ESV)

But he didn't say God made the universe with his arm—or even his hand. He said, "God, you made it with your fingers!"

The vast universe is so small to God that for him it's like making a toy model—with just his fingers!

If the Milky Way galaxy were the size of North America, our solar system would be a coffee cup, and earth would be a speck of dust inside the cup.

The universe is tiny to God!

What are human beings next to God? Nothing!

And yet God says you fill his mind.

 Illustration by Jago

"I remember the first time I come across it. Was a two-month sail out of Valetta. I was laid up ugly for near-about three week with a mean bout o' the shivery-sweats. Laid hold o' the finest book aboard and settled onto some right fine readin' time, see here? There's good bits for readin' in the hills of that there mole. Good bits indeed."
—Bartimaeus Gann, Able Seaman (WNI)

62

FIXING THE BROKEN RECORD
by Jason Gray

On the wall of my friend Cason's house, there's a picture of him holding his newborn son. They are staring at one another, each with an astonished look that is both funny and poignant: a child, newly arrived on planet earth, trying to make sense of where he's landed, and a young man holding what seems like the weight of the world in a seven-pound baby boy. Our friend Tyler looked at the picture and said to Cason, "This is the one where he's looking at you and saying, 'who *are* you?' and you're looking back at him and saying, 'who *am* I?'"

The joke, like the picture, is both funny and poignant, naming the fundamental question we ask ourselves every moment of our lives. We're like broken records with a scratch so deep the needle can't jump the groove; the question keeps coming at us, playing over and over again until it fades into the white noise of everyday life. *Who am I?*, it whispers. After a while, we don't pay attention to it anymore—though it never stops demanding an answer.

But from time to time it emerges from the background. We hear it most clearly in life's defining moments (like weddings and funerals) or during periods of self-doubt (like when a father holds his newborn son), but the question is always rising up out of the great mystery of self, whether we note it or not: *Who am I? Who am I? Who am I? . . .*

In one of his most famous stories, Jesus tells a parable that could stand as the summation of human history. The scene opens with a loving father and his two sons, and we sense right away that this is no ordinary father—that Jesus is speaking of his heavenly father: perfect, loving, "slow to anger, abounding in love . . ." (Ex. 34:6 NIV). And yet, there appears to be division and heartbreak in the home. We're not far into the story when the younger son, who has seemingly had it up to "here," decides to go in search of himself, believing he'll find what he's looking for in a distant land, far from his father's house. How did this bitter division come into the family, especially under the roof of such a loving father?

In 2010, I was part of an artists' retreat in East Tennessee where author John Sheasby—a stocky, white-haired, walking burst of joy with an irresistible South African accent—spoke to us about the place we hold in the heart of God the Father. Sheasby is a man so alive with the love of God that he makes others thirsty for whatever he's drunk on.

His text was Luke 15, the story of the lost son, and he spent the week persuading us of our *Birthright* (the title of his book) and the difference between understanding ourselves as "servants" of God and understanding ourselves as "sons and daughters" of God—a fundamental difference that shapes every part of our lives.

Consider the servant: he lives on the estate, but in separate quarters, apart from the master and his family. However, this is the lesser measure of the distance between them, the greater being not so much a matter of proximity as it is of condition: the servant-master relationship is dependent upon performance. The servant's position is secure only insofar as he meets the expectations of his master. He may be dutiful and devoted, but the servant shares no real familiarity with his master because his place in the household is ultimately conditional.

A son, on the other hand, lives in his father's house, not in the servants' quarters but in the fine rooms of the master's family. He's secure in his position because of who he *is* and not what he *does*. He and his father enjoy one another's company,

64

sometimes laughing together, other times crying together. They share inside jokes and an easy intimacy. And though the son may desire to please his father, he knows it's not a condition of the relationship. Nothing he does will change the fact that he is a *son*, dearly loved.

Loving, and being loved by, a father is wholly different from serving a master. This simple delineation between servant and son helps us see what might be happening in our own hearts. When we think like a servant it cripples our ability to both receive and give love. We fashion an invisible measuring stick and carry it around with us everywhere we go, continually measuring ourselves against it to determine our standing. We believe our place in our master's household is assured only to the degree that we imagine we are pleasing him, so we anxiously focus on our performance, making our list and checking it twice. We become handwringers whose assurances are tenuous at best.

The real problem with carrying a measuring stick around all the time is that we continually feel measured by it. It's always there, accusing and shaming us (as well as everyone around us—others feel measured by it also). Over time, we forget that the measuring stick is a thing of our *own* making, and we begin blaming our feelings of inadequacy on those we had hoped to please.

And so the story goes that a son gradually begins to believe that he is a servant, until one day he decides he's had enough and turns his measuring stick into a walking stick. "I'm tired of trying to live up to your demands, old man. I can never be good enough for you!" He leaves with a vengeance, demanding his inheritance, in essence saying, "Your money is all that matters to me, and I can't wait for you to die." The conflict inside him has reached the boiling point; it spills over and burns those who love him most.

There was a young girl I once knew who often fell into the wrong kind of relationships. Deep in her heart lived the lie that she didn't deserve to be treated with honor. It was confusing for her when a man would come along who actually treated her with respect and kindness, because she didn't know how to interpret it. She would say that something about him made her feel "bad" or "uncomfortable." Inevitably, she would return to abusive relationships because those, at least, made some kind of sense to her. It wasn't until she was able to believe in God's inherent love for her that she began to heal and the course of her life began to change.

I believe this is what's at work in the heart of the younger son. His own sense of unworthiness foils his capacity to receive love and rises up inside him to accuse his father of being impossible to please. Shame distorts even love until it feels like a demand, and so he casts himself away from the very love that could heal him. But where does his deep sense of unworthiness come from? And where will it take him?

Proverbs 4:23 cautions man to be mindful of his heart because it is the "wellspring of life." The writer is telling us that whatever is in our hearts will determine the course of our lives. And so when we find ourselves in places we never wanted to go, it is our own hearts that we must look to and ask what it is that's driving us. We all have regrets, but are we driven into shame by sin? Or are we driven into sin by our shame? Is shame a consequence? Or is it a pre-existing condition? If it was there to begin with, how did it get there? And how can it be unseated?

The Bible begins with a story much like the one Jesus tells in Luke 15. There's a Father and his beloved children. The children live and play in a garden and are well provided for, without a thing to fear in the world. Though they are naked, they are unashamed, covered by the Father's perfect love. All is well until the children believe a lie; they're told that their Father does not *really* love them and has withheld something good from them. In the moment they doubt their Father's love, they reject the goodness of the life he's provided and reach for a life of their own making. They disobey the one decree of the garden and eat from the Tree of the Knowledge of Good and Evil—a decision that unleashes a curse on the entire world. The knowledge they gain brings with it shame over their naked vulnerability and infects them with fear: fear of the world, fear of each other, even fear of their loving Father.

The curse spills over their hearts and into the soil that once rewarded the work of their hands with bountiful harvests. From this point forward, the ground will resist the labor they give to it. It's this tragic futility that still haunts us, their great grandchildren, and reaches beyond the garden to touch everything we put our hands and hearts to. We are plagued with a sense of ineffectuality as our efforts are frustrated, not producing what they ought to. We often feel that no matter what we do, it's not enough. We fear that perhaps *we* aren't enough—as spouses, as parents, as providers, as friends, as children of God. This fundamental sense of futility is the pebble in our shoe that troubles every step of our way.

The curse of futility has left humanity with an embarrassing impotence that causes us to doubt our worth. Maybe Augustine would have called it "original shame." This deep wound of insecurity drives us to look for assurances of worth wherever they may be found: wealth, sex, power, status. Like a black hole that consumes everything we try to fill it with, it's the scratch in the record that won't let the needle move off of the question of "Who am I?" We may demand assurances of worth from our spouses, from our children, or from our careers or trophy cases, but the question keeps coming at us, and it's never satisfied. How many CEOs, athletes, leaders, performers, or outstanding achievers of any stripe are driven by that one question? How many ever find a truly enduring answer?

There are others who manage the wound by running away from the question—hiding in endless sensual distractions, addictions, or detached resignation. The majority of us, however, navigate a course between the two extremes, driven neither to achievement nor lassitude, obeying our shame through desperate grabs at significance one moment and medicating it the next. Here in the exile of our self-imposed rejection, we are led away by a lie that tempts us to believe that our Father is now a judge who sees us as we see ourselves.

So it is that it's not only earthen soil that's subject to the curse of futility; it's also the soil of our hearts. A tangle of thorn and weeds, it resists the work of the loving hands of our Father. But he knows how to grow beautiful things from even the most difficult ground, and though our shame drives us far from home, there remains a seed he has buried deep within us: the memory of the goodness of a Father's love.

The young son flees to a far-off land where he surrounds himself with admirers, finding all the assurance of worth that money can buy. He's the life of the party, medicating his shame with sex, debauchery, and every mode of escapism available. But there's not enough money in the world to heal the festering wound of insecurity in the human heart, and one day the money runs out along with the conditional love of his new friends. The shadowy lie he believed about his father's rejection now grows into a gaping darkness that swallows him whole. It's a tragic, self-fulfilling prophecy.

Destitute, pathetic, and utterly abandoned, he takes the only work he can get: feeding someone else's pigs. He's so poor that he longs to eat the slop of the animals he feeds. The truth he's been running from has finally caught up to him with a force that topples him over, plunging him deep into the wound of his own shame.

Who am I? Who am I? Who am I? . . .

It's there in the pit that one word slowly comes to him, forming in his mind and heart like a solitary tongue of flame that is just enough to keep the darkness from overwhelming him completely. The word is "home."

What happens next is revealing, I think, because what he remembers about home exposes the lie that's been living in his heart all along.

"When he came to his senses, he said, 'How many of my father's hired *servants* (emphasis mine) have food to spare, and here I am starving to death!" (Lk. 15:17 NIV). His mind turns first not to his father's love, but to the thought of his father's servants! The lie still holds sway, but for now it's enough that he's roused. He drops the pail of pig slop and turns homeward.

It's a long journey, but it gives him time to rehearse the speech that he hopes will soften his father's heart and change his fortune. One foot in front of the other, he stumbles along, looking for just the right words: "Father, I have sinned against heaven and against you; I am no longer worthy to be called your son; make me like one of your hired servants" (Lk. 15:18–19 NIV). The son is rehearsing the speech of a servant. He may have reached the end of himself, but he still doesn't know his true identity.

On he walks. He crosses the border into the land where he grew up, the land that raised him out of the earth like a strong stalk of wheat, and as if waking from a strange dream, life returns to him. His heart lightens as he rounds a bend and comes upon the familiar scenery of his youth. There's the hill he used to climb as a boy! There's the field where he laid on his back with his older brother to count the stars. There are the familiar trees that his father taught him the names for.

Father. The word weighs like a stone on his heart, and the life that had rushed back into him at the sight of his homeland recedes into shadow again. His feet feel heavy. They drag across the gravel, weighted down by the dread of seeing the old man whose heart he's broken. What will his father say? What will he find in his father's eyes? The wayward son remembers the last words between them, so empowering and so righteous at the time, but now so dull, tarnished by experience and regret. All at once, his shame is the only thing he believes about himself and the whole world. He begins mumbling his speech again, desperate for the right words—words that might save him, words that might build a bridge across the raging watercourse of his guilt.

Though he's the loneliest man in the world, he's not alone. The wound runs deep in all of us, all the way to the very beginning, when a boy and girl played in a garden, naked and unashamed, unknowing of the knowledge of good and evil. Before the Fall, were Adam and Eve innocent in the same way children are, who are able to love and be loved in a way that is near to perfection? How quickly a child is able to forgive and accept that they are forgiven, giving themselves freely to those they love. How many times have I scolded my own children, only to have them climb into my lap moments later, holding me, fearless, bearing no grudge? Though children whine and fuss, they never doubt the love of their parents. They are blessedly free of reticence. Is it a quality of innocence that is not yet spoiled by the full-blown knowledge of good and evil?

As we get older, we grow into this knowledge; it excites our fear and cripples us with doubt. We learn to cover our nakedness and protect ourselves. Though Adam and Eve had been naked all along, it wasn't until they ate the fruit of the Tree of the Knowledge of Good and Evil that they *knew* they were naked, implying that sin is more than merely an act we commit; it's a broken way of knowing ourselves and the world. At least in some measure, their condition wasn't changed so much as was their knowledge of it. And they were ashamed ever after. Because fear follows closely on the heels of shame, they ran and hid from God. We, their descendants, heirs of the curse, have been doing the same ever since.

But beneath this terrible knowledge, we are still beloved children who, more than anything, need to come out of our hiding places and return to our Father's house to dwell in his presence and be named and healed by his love. The knowledge of our sin, however, tempts us to run from the One we need the most. Shame becomes the ultimate idolatry, exalting the knowledge of our sin above the knowledge of who our Father is: "slow to anger, abounding in love..."

So a son comes to imagine himself an unworthy servant, rejecting his own birthright, his own belovedness, thus believing himself rejected. The lie in his heart puts him on a course that takes him far from his father's house, into the furthest reaches of his own pain, before spitting him out into the gutter. But it's here that the depth of his shame finally surfaces and with it the possibility of healing. As he makes his way back home, he prepares a servant's speech—but it's a speech that will fail him beautifully.

In this passage of scripture, Jesus gives us one of the most startling images of God that we've ever seen, an image too good to not be true:

> But while he was still a long way off, his father saw him and was filled with compassion for him; he ran to his son, threw his arms around him and kissed him.
>
> The son said to him, "Father, I have sinned against heaven and against you. I am no longer worthy to be called your son."
>
> But the father said to his servants, "Quick! Bring the best robe and put it on him. Put a ring on his finger and sandals on his feet. Bring the fattened calf and kill it. Let's have a feast and celebrate. For this son of mine was dead and is alive again; he was lost and is found." So they began to celebrate. (Lk. 15:20–24 NIV)

There is so much beauty in this moment that it's easy to miss the particular beauty of the way the son isn't allowed to finish his speech—he had intended to beg his father for employment as a servant, but his father won't even let him get that far, silencing the plea before it's ever spoken. The plea is all that the boy has dwelled on for his long journey home, perhaps believing his very salvation depended upon it. But he has barely begun when the words he has so carefully prepared are interrupted by a single word from his father: "Quick!" This one word is a powerful dismissal of the shame that has held the boy's heart captive. *There is no more time to give to this notion!* So: *Quick! Get a robe, a ring, and sandals. This* son *of mine was dead and is alive again!* With a word, the lie is brushed aside and the question of his identity is answered by the love of his father. In the moment he is most exposed, he is held, sheltered, and named, clothed in the raiment of a son.

Quick! My boy, my child who I love, was lost and is found again! He has come home!

At the beginning of the story, Jesus told us there were two sons, and with the dramatic return of the younger son, the narrative turns to his brother.

> Meanwhile, the older son was in the field. When he came near the house, he heard music and dancing. So he called one of the servants and asked him what was going on. "Your brother has come," he replied, "and your father has killed the fattened calf because he has him back safe and sound." (Lk. 15:25—26)

Just as the one son is returning through the front door, the other has gone out the back and refuses to join the party. The Father goes to him, just as he did to the younger brother, and asks him to come inside.

> But he answered his father, "Look! All these years I've been slaving for you and never disobeyed your orders. Yet you never gave me even a young goat so I could celebrate with my friends. But when this son of yours who has squandered your property with prostitutes comes home, you kill the fattened calf for him!" (Lk. 15:29–30 NIV)

Though he's the son who stayed, we find that he is just as lost as his younger brother and all the more tragically for his self-assured ignorance of it. Maybe he never left, but he's never made himself at home in his father's house either. Blinded by his own apparent goodness, he's like the man Jesus speaks of in Luke 18 who entered the temple praying, "I thank you, God, that I am not a sinner like everyone else. For I don't cheat, I don't sin, and I don't commit adultery." When the question of "Who am I?" rises up in the elder brother, he answers with who he isn't: "I'm certainly not like my younger brother!"

Though it's expressed differently, he is inflicted with the same servant mindset as his brother. Look at his language: "I've been *slaving* for you . . ." he seethes, thrusting out his measuring stick. "See! See all my effort! See how hard I've tried to please you, and yet it was never enough to warrant even a small goat!"

Absent without leaving, he's an angry man, consumed from the inside out with the slow-burning contempt of self-righteousness; his heart is a bed of smoldering ashes. But wait! Here, finally, is a brief conflagration—a sign of life!—and with it a chance for healing. The father answers his boy's angry accusation with a loving affirmation of his sonship.

"My son," the father said, "you are always with me, and everything I have is yours. But we had to celebrate and be glad, because this brother of yours was dead and is alive again; he was lost and is found." (Lk. 15:31–32 NIV)

Such gentleness! "Everything I have is yours," the father says. But the voice of the servant runs so deep in his son that you wonder if he can even hear the words. The elder brother's is the story of those of us who live in the Father's house but aren't able to enjoy all he's provided. We insist on earning what is already ours and are angry when we discover we *can't* earn it. Sick with the same sense of unworthiness as the younger brother, we medicate and manage it not with wild living, but instead with a calculated, joyless, and self-righteous sense of duty. Unable to enjoy grace or its furnishings, love becomes conscription and the father's desire for closeness an unyielding demand. If only the elder brother could rest in the affection of his father, he might enjoy what is already his and learn to give himself away in love rather than out of cheerless obligation.

The needless suffering of his children breaks the father's heart, and for all the ways they refuse his love—either by running away or by hiding behind their own carefully measured righteousness—he still longs to be close to them. He comes out to both of them, to meet them and bring them home. Jesus never tells us what the elder son decides, but I'm left with a sense that the father's heart will be broken again.

"You are always with me, and everything I have is yours." Will the boy hear and understand?

Pastor and author Tim Keller has spoken at length on this passage and how the two sons represent the two ways we look for both happiness and an answer to the question of "Who am I?" The younger brother takes the path of self-discovery while the elder takes the path of moral conformity. Both lead, quite literally, to a dead end.

The way of self-discovery tries to fill the open wound of shame with a lust for unfettered freedom, feeding emptiness with restless wandering and the distraction of new adventures. For those who go this way, self-expression and accumulated experience are their measuring sticks. *Carpe diem* is their rallying cry, and strewn in their wake are the broken hearts of those who love them.

The way of moral conformity tries to manage shame through the grim observance of moral conviction. Anxious measurers of both their own virtues and everyone else's, they are faithful to the letter, though the words no longer sing. They are dutiful, but they have forgotten they are in a love story. They are a walking testament to the verse that says, "...for the letter kills, but the Spirit gives life." (2 Cor. 3:6 NKJV)

The accoutrements of these parallel crises of identity—freedom, self-expression, faithfulness, duty, etc.—are beautiful in and of themselves, but our shame and our misguided pursuit of a sense of worth ruin them and every other good thing in our lives.

I am either of these sons at any given time, and though it may be easier to spot waywardness in others, it's myself that I am accountable for. Comparison may be the thief of joy, but it's also the thief of self-knowledge, and we'll never find healing for the wound in ourselves as long as we're always pointing at the wound in others. So Jesus tells me to be mindful of my *own* heart, to look after the beam in my *own* eye. So it goes for each of us. If you can't see the beam, it's probably safe to assume it's blinding you. Ask the Holy Spirit to reveal it. Repeatedly.

That being said, most of us probably have either a younger or an elder "son" in our own lives whom we worry over and who we fear may break our hearts. What can we do? How can we protect both them and ourselves from pain? Do we try to help them see the futility of their lustful pursuits of self-discovery? Do we point out the vanity of their quests for moral-conformity?

I don't think so. Conviction is the domain of the Holy Spirit, and presuming to venture into His territory usually only makes matters worse. Though there are times when we may be led to confront the waywardness in another, we are often too eager to do so and forget that only the Spirit of God can reveal brokenness in a way that brings life, and, even then, only when a person is able to receive it. No, the story is clear. It may be that the best we can do is to love generously, knowing that there's no way to protect ourselves from the pain of loving. Then we wait. And if we're lucky enough to see the wayward one come home again, we run out to meet him. And if a speech is offered, there may be no words more healing than, "Quick! Ready the party! The one I love was lost and is found!"

There is also a third son to be considered: the one who is telling us the story. The third son, of course, is Jesus, and in him we see the son we all wish to be and the promise of the son we may become. Though our shame has driven us far from our Father's house, Jesus, our brother, finds us in the far off land and comes to persuade us of a truth so beautiful that our fearful hearts can barely let it in: that we are more than mere servants, that we are sons and daughters, that we are loved.

His is the voice that comes to us in our destitution and whispers "home." He is the solitary flame in the overwhelming darkness at the end of our selves. He is both the road that leads us home and our companion as we walk the road. His presence refutes the words of the servant speeches we rehearse along the way. His is the voice in the field of our labor, bringing news of the great mercy of the Father who receives wayward sons. He asks us to see the beauty of the Father who "does not treat us as our sins deserve or repay us according to our iniquities" (Ps. 103:10 NIV). "Because of the Lord's great love we are not consumed, for his compassions never fail!" (Lam. 3:22 NIV). He prays for us as the Father approaches and asks us to abandon our labor and come inside.

Jesus and our Father conspire together to "rescue us from the dominion of darkness" (Col. 1:13 NIV) and bring us back to our Father's house. Jesus comes to restore us as sons and daughters, to heal the wound of original shame, and answer with decisive finality the question of our worth. There is no depth to which Jesus will not descend to prove the Father's love. He has taken our measuring sticks and fashioned out of them a cross.

> . . . he humbled himself
> by becoming obedient to death—
> even death on a cross! (Phil. 2:8 NIV)

In Jesus we see the love of God that fills the scratch in the record so that the needle finally moves on. "Who am I?" we ask? We are answered: "To all who did receive him, who believed in his name, he gave the right to become children of God . . ." (Jn. 1:12 ESV). "So you are no longer a slave, but God's child; and since you are his child, God has made you also an heir" (Gal. 4:7 NIV). And "because you are his sons, God sent the Spirit of his Son into our hearts, the Spirit who calls out, 'Abba, Father'" (Gal. 4:6 NIV).

Who are we? We are servants no longer. We are sons, daughters, beloved children of God. As we turn toward home we are met by our Father who runs to receive us, saying: *Quick! Waste no more time trying to prove your worth. Come home and let my love for you be proven instead! See, I have engraved your name on the palm of my hand, and I have removed your sins as far from us as the east is from the west. Let me cover your nakedness, let my love cast out your fear, let us celebrate, for my child was lost and is now found!*

ρλˈínɟσơ ρλíмɥ ɟúɣ ρλɜ̃ ˜ɯ̃ɟɛ̀lɟɟɟɛ̀ ρlˈ ρɯ̃jᵇ αlˈ ˈɟ̃рɛ́ íɱҏᴉ̀ɣ ƥ

—Legolas (WNI)

JESUS AND THE DRAGON QUEST

by Travis Prinzi*

I procrastinate badly whenever I have something to write. Before sitting down to write this essay, my distraction was *Dragon Quest VI*, a role playing game for Nintendo. Why this confession? I've been playing *Dragon Quest* games since I was in the second grade. The reason I'm drawn to them is that I get to become a participant in the story. I name the main character after myself, and after sixty or seventy hours of what many people would call a waste of time, I've saved an imaginary world from imaginary monsters.

Everyone loves to tell stories. But there's a difference between telling a story you heard and telling a story that you were in. *Dragon Quest* is a story I'm in.

And so is the Gospel.

Most people consider fairy tales and fantasy fiction to be cute little stories, completely untrue, that are used to teach kids moral lessons. This is not at all what a fairy tale truly is, as wise people like G.K. Chesterton once understood:

> My first and last philosophy, that which I believe in with unbroken certainty, I learnt in the nursery. I generally learnt it from a nurse; that is, from

---

*Illustrations by Justin Gerard. Sketches on pages 78 and 84 are developmental stages of the final illustration on page 91. See the completed painting, "St. George & the Dragon No. 8," at www.JustinGerard.com. All images © 2012 Justin Gerard.

the solemn and star-appointed priestess at once of democracy and tradi-
tion. The things I believed most then, the things I believe most now, are
the things called fairy tales. They seem to me to be the entirely reasonable
things. They are not fantasies: compared with them other things are fan-
tastic. (*Orthodoxy*)

Fairy tales teach us more than simple moral lessons; they teach us a philosophy
about the world. They tell us that, as Chesterton puts it, the world is a wild and star-
tling place. The fairy tale taught Chesterton that the world was dynamic and full of
magic. This is in contrast to the "scientific fatalist" who believes that the world oper-
ates strictly on fixed laws and cannot possibly have been any other way than exactly
the way it is. Fairy tales tell us, instead, that the world is not merely a machine, but
a changing and exciting place, with heroes and villains and tales of treachery and
courage. And yes, magic.

How does the fairy tale communicate its philosophy? J. R. R. Tolkien's essay "On
Fairy-Stories" provides important insight into the nature and workings of the fairy
tale. The world of Faerie was every bit as important to Tolkien's thought as it was to
Chesterton's. According to Tolkien, the fairy tale provides four gifts to the reader:
Fantasy, Recovery, Escape, and Consolation. These gifts are at the heart of the fairy tale's
ability to communicate truth about the world.

Fantasy

The term "fantasy" is often used to denote that genre for only the weirdest of geeks who dress up like their heroes, wear wizard's robes, carry around swords, and go to odd conventions. In other words, its mention is usually accompanied by an eye-roll so forceful that there may well be documented cases of blindness-by-condescension-toward-fantasy-lovers.

But Fantasy, Tolkien argues, is "not a lower but a higher form of art, indeed the most nearly pure form." Great news for the geeks among us. But why is this so?

Fantasy is the ultimate act of sub-creation because one has to create an entire Secondary World that is different from the Primary World in which we live but is as entirely internally consistent. This is difficult work because the Secondary World must be consistent enough to command what Tolkien calls "Secondary Belief."

Against those who think that Fantasy is either a waste of time or even that it is evil—because it creates a "lie" (a story that didn't happen)—Tolkien argues that Fantasy is "a natural human activity" because, being made in the image of a creative God, making things is a reflection of the way that we are, ourselves, made. The Fall may have damaged us severely and caused distortions in our creative activity, but our right and our inclination to create is not lost, and in Christ, it may be redeemed. God created a world; Christ created us anew; we create secondary worlds.

I began my book, *Harry Potter and Imagination* (Zossima 2008), with a quote from a Christian man complaining thusly about the Harry Potter stories and fiction in general:

> "I recommend that people stop wasting their time reading fiction (lies) for entertainment, and that parents teach their children by good example to spend more time reading wholesome nonfiction with literary value (including the Bible) for education."

To that, I think a traditional fairy-tale ending is a sufficient counter-argument. We're used to "and they lived happily ever after," but another traditional ending went like this:

The Dreamer awakes
The shadow goes by
The tale I have told you,
That tale is a lie.
But listen to me,
Bright maiden, proud youth
The tale is a lie;
What it tells is the truth.

"They are not lies," Tolkien said to C. S. Lewis, when the latter used that label for myths. By "they are not lies," Tolkien wasn't saying: "These myths literally happened." He was saying: "What they tell is the truth." The traditional folk-tale ending is saying: "Sure, this tale did not actually happen; but it still tells you the truth"—the deeper truths of life, the truth about love and sacrifice.

"The notion that motor cars are more 'alive' than, say, centaurs or dragons is curious," Tolkien wrote in "On Fairy-Stories." We fill the world around us with all kinds of things that are not real, and then we call it the real world. This is what Tolkien is getting at. We tend to tacitly assume that the way things are around us is just the way reality is. We then christen it "The Real World" and scoff at anything that doesn't look like the technological grid we've built around us. Fantasy jars us from this grid and points us to magic—magic that is older than the world itself.

Fantasy is a gift of the true fairy-story because the desire, ability, and right to create is a gift from God, and through our creating, we communicate truth about God.

RECOVERY

Tolkien called "Recovery" the "regaining of a clear view." From what do we need Recovery? From familiarity leading to boredom—the false view that every leaf is just the same, that the world is mundane and drab. This was why Chesterton valued fairy tales so highly—not because they were an escape from reality, but because they taught him the way that he should think about reality, which was much different than a mechanistic view. This is what Coleridge meant by obtaining a Transformed Vision, an ability to see with the "eye of the heart."

Philip Doddridge wrote in his advent hymn, "Hark the Glad Sound":

> He comes from thickest films of vice
> To clear the mental ray
> And on the eyes oppressed by night
> To pour celestial day

The Fall distorted our clear view of God, of ourselves, and of the world. It caused us to know good and evil when all we were intended to know was the goodness of God. We can no longer see the world rightly because we can no longer see God. On Sinai, Moses was not permitted to look at God. Only in his incarnation as a human being can we see God again rightly. God Incarnate said:

> Your eye is a lamp that provides light for your body. When your eye is good, your whole body is filled with light. But when your eye is bad, your whole body is filled with darkness. And if the light you think you have is actually darkness, how deep that darkness! (Mt. 6:22–23 NLT)

Our problem is one of vision. The light we think we have is actually darkness. Coleridge, Tolkien, Lewis, and others believed that a good fairy tale can provide recovery of sight—the ability to better see the world for what it is.[1] Fairy-stories train the eyes of the heart to see spiritually.

---

[1] This is not to say that the fairy tale can do what Christ does. Spiritual vision is only truly and fully opened by Jesus. But the fairy tale can shed some light where there was none before.

ESCAPE

You've probably heard the notion that stories are for "escaping" or for entertainment value. Some suggest that a page-turner is all we want—something that will help us to veg out, to leave the day behind. I like entertainment just as much as anyone else, but a line often gets crossed in this type of thinking, and criticism is turned on those who believe there is more to storytelling than mindless fun. The argument usually goes something like this: "Authors don't have imaginative keys to their works. They're not keeping secrets. You're just looking for a Da Vinci Code or something. You're looking for some secret gnostic meaning."

The reason I think this crosses a line is that the one who quickly dismisses, out-of-hand, the possibility that books have deeper levels of meaning, claiming that authors write exciting books just for the profit and fun of it all, is insulting the craft of writing and storytelling. Why is it the default assumption that authors don't have imaginative keys to their work? Why is the author, by default, put in the role of mindless entertainer, instead of careful artist?

It's important that we distinguish between "escape" from the world for mindless entertainment and Tolkien's idea of fairy-tale Escape. The escape of mindless-fun is the mentality mentioned above: authors write quick-paced stories for profit, and we escape our real lives for a little while in order to stop thinking about the world and feed ourselves on entertainment junk food. Paradoxically, this is often considered a good thing, because we all need a break from reality, which is cruel and difficult. Others meet this notion of escape with criticism. Detaching oneself from reality is not a good thing; in fact, it's childish, some would say.

Tolkien's response to this kind of mindless-fun escape is to argue that this mentality springs from the false belief (explained in the previous section) that current trends define Real Life. The electric street lamp, for example, is nowhere near as permanent as lightning, but most of us know more about the lamp because it's more relevant to our daily existence.

Instead, Tolkien speaks of Escape in a much different way:

Why should a man be scorned, if, finding himself in a prison, he tries to get out and go home? Or if, when he cannot do so, he thinks and talks about other topics than jailers and prison-walls? ("On Fairy-Stories")

The fairy tale Escape takes us to the lightning itself, the more permanent thing. Escape allows us to talk about other topics than the tragedy of the fallen world (the "prison") we live in. Fairy tale Escape is rooted in our longing for home, our desire to no longer be subject to the curse and to catch a glimpse of the final defeat of evil and the triumph of good in the pages of a magical story. When we're on the dragon quest, we're escaping not from the Real World, but to a place that puts us in contact with themes and symbols in a cohesive, magical world that tells us about our own and gives us glimpses of what this world could and should be.

What Escape ultimately does is put us in touch with our ancient human desires. We desire an escape from our present circumstance because we know that something is wrong, that the world is a mess, and that we were designed for something better. We want to go there, and so we write and read stories that bring us as close as our fallen minds can get to imagining it.

We seek the dragon, whether willingly, like in my video game, or reluctantly, like Bilbo, because the fairy tale taught us, as children, that dragons can be defeated— and we want to defeat one. We want to escape the dragon's curse.

CONSOLATION

The real power of the fairy tale, and the most potent of its gifts, is that of Consolation, especially the Happy Ending, as Tolkien says. His term *eucatastrophe* refers to that "good catastrophe," the "sudden joyous turn"; it is the surprising event in which, out of the seemingly inevitable victory of evil over good, evil is defeated and good wins. To return to my video game analogy, my favorite battles in *Dragon Quest* and similar games have been those in which, entire party fallen and my character on his last bit of strength, I deal the final blow to the evil overlord. I realize how nerdy

that sounds. But it's a very small picture, or icon, of the kind of joy provided by the Consolation of the fairy story.

It's because of this that Tolkien can make the following conclusion: "The Gospels contain a fairy story, or a story of a larger kind which embraces all the essence of fairy-stories."

You're in a Fairy Tale

"You best start believing in ghost stories, Miss Turner. You're in one."

Those words are spoken by Captain Barbossa, the cursed pirate captain in the movie *Pirates of the Caribbean*. We could take the same sentiment and turn it on those who are skeptical of the power of fairy tales.

Tolkien believed that the story of Christ is a fairy tale that "has entered History and the Primary World." By our fairy-stories, we show our desire to return to the world for which we were created, to be freed from the curse of the Fall, and to satisfy our "ancient human desires." But at the Incarnation, all the imaginative desire of the fairy tale came into being here in the Real World, the world of street lamps and motorcars. The Happy Ending has arrived. The Dragon has been defeated and will suffer a final blow in the end.

The fairy tale, then, is not some silly story that we put away with other childish things, but a glimpse of the one true fairy-story. And if the Christ story is a fairy-story, then the surprise for all of us is that we are actually characters in it.

There's a moment in *The Hobbit*, another story of a dragon quest, when a small town is confronted with a fairy tale come to life, much like we are with the realization that the Jesus tale is true. Let's follow Bilbo's story for a moment. Pay close attention to the reactions of the people of Lake-town, who have heard all about the legend that is about to appear on their doorstep but have always treated it much in the same way that we treat our own fairy tales.

Bilbo starts the story comfortable in the Shire with no plans of adventure. He is suddenly thrown, partially against his will, into an adventure with a band of

85

dwarves and a quirky wizard. He escapes trolls, goblins, Gollum, spiders, and wood-elves; he discovers a magic ring and a sword. At this point, about two-thirds of the way into the book, Tolkien makes a very deliberate story transition: "...we are now drawing near the end of the eastward journey and coming to the last and greatest adventure, so we must hurry on" (Chapter 9, "Barrels Out of Bond").

From there, we step into Lake-town, a small village of people a few days from Dale and the Lonely Mountain, dwarf dwelling places that were destroyed by the dragon, Smaug. The dwarves are returning to reclaim their treasure and defeat Smaug. In Lake-town, a fascinating little legend (or fairy tale) had been told for many years. The tale said that the Dwarf kings Thror and Thrain would return "and gold would flow in rivers through the mountain-gates, and all that land would be filled with new song and new laughter." In other words, the tale claims that a land plunged into darkness by an evil dragon would be returned to a state of glory by the return of a king. You hear, I'm sure, the echoes of the Gospel tale in that.

As we journey with Bilbo, King Thorin, and the other dwarves, we are journeying *with* the fairy tale into the land in need of magic. And here's how we're received. There are five distinct responses to the fairy tale by the people of Lake-town:

The first response: "But this pleasant legend did not much affect their daily business." This editorial comment by Tolkien in Chapter 10 describes the way most of the world responds to the old magic, the true magic of the one true fairy tale. It doesn't much affect our daily business. Fairy tales are simply dismissed as silly children's tales, nursery rhymes meant to teach kids to behave. They have no bearing on the lives of many people, and indeed, it would be considered foolish to let them affect Real Life. A fairy tale might be a nice story to be made into an interesting movie, but it has no bearing on one's ability to pay the bills or find a decent vacation home. So why bother with them? These are the folks who hold everything from indifference to disdain for believers in fairy tales.

The second response: "Some of the more foolish ran out of the hut as if they expected the Mountain to go golden in the night and all the waters of the lake to turn yellow right away." Some, in other words, thought that the redemption of the land would happen in an instant, as though a simple magic spell would instantly do away with all evil. There are at least two faults here: a certain gullible disposition that will believe almost anything, and a miscalculation about the devastation caused by Smaug. Smaug's evil was too great to be undone because a few dwarves simply walked into town. In the same way, some do not take adequate stock of the extent, depth, and power of the Fall. They think that Jesus just makes everything okay in an instant. As Tolkien reminds us about the fairy tale, the Happy Ending does not deny the fact that sorrow and failure are still regular parts of our story, and at times defeat seems almost inevitable.

The third response: "The Elvenking was very powerful in those parts and the Master wished for no enmity with him, nor did he think much of old songs, giving his mind to trade and tolls, to cargoes and gold, to which habit he owed his position." The "Master," the ruler of Lake-town, was far too concerned with money, power, and privilege to pay any attention to old songs and tales that might change things. To some it doesn't matter what kind of suffering and tragedy happens, or what kind of redemption or change might be possible, as long as one's own power stays intact.

The fourth response: "It was easier to believe in the Dragon and less easy to believe in Thorin in these wild parts." In the shadow of the Lonely Mountain, the effects of Smaug's evil actions were so potent that it was very difficult, near impossible, to have hope or trust in old tales. The man about whom this statement was made was standing in the presence of Thorin, the very fulfillment of the legend, but believed more in the terror of Smaug than in the tale. This is the exact opposite of the foolish response above, which took Smaug's evil lightly. Those that respond to the fairy tale in this way are so affected by evil and the Fall and all the terror it has caused that hope seems an impossibility.

The fifth response, of course, is that of Bilbo and the dwarves themselves. They believe the story because they're in it. They continue on with their dragon quest. They approach the mountain and finish the story. They are the tale itself, and they are quite true. The legend told in Lake-town comes to pass through Bilbo and the dwarves. Fairy tales, you see, won't stop existing because someone disbelieves them. The story goes on. The tale retains its potency. The magic still works. The gospel heals and saves even its strongest opponents and radical disbelievers. Dragons are slain because hobbits and dwarves believe they can be, and they press on.

Years later, in his conversation with Gandalf and Balin, Bilbo is surprised to hear that the old tales, songs, and prophecies have come true.

"Of course!" says Gandalf. "And why should they not prove true? Surely you don't disbelieve the prophecies, because you had a hand in bringing them about yourself? You don't really suppose, do you, that all your adventures and escapes were managed by mere luck, just for your sole benefit?"

As with Bilbo, so with us in our response to the great Fairy Tale, the True Myth. We get to enter into it and be part of the story.

Fairy Tales are True

So where does this leave us in response to fairy tales? Do we still need them, since we know there is one true tale? Why bother with the echoes? There are two clear reasons that we should highly value fairy tales and fantasy stories.

The first is that as humans created in the image and likeness of a creator, it's a good and natural and normal activity for us to create our own worlds. We are sub-creators, Tolkien says. Because we are made in the image of God the Creator, it is a natural human inclination to create. And without any disrespect meant to other arts, the creation of an entire Secondary World—an Elfland or a Fairyland—is as close as humans get to the original creative activity of God, what Tolkien calls the "most pure" form of art. When creating Fairyland, sub-creators tap into primordial human desires (our longing for restoration) by painting pictures of Eden. Tolkien notes the ability to communicate with other living things (a pre-Fall image from Genesis) as an example. We can use the creative imagination to stir up longing for redemption and give glimpses of it in the story's *eucatastrophe*.

The second reason for valuing fairy tales is that story teaches us how to think about the world around us. It opens up the opportunity for the transformed vision, the recovery that Tolkien spoke of, "regaining a clear view."

Lewis gives us some help here:

> . . . only Supernaturalists really see Nature. You must go a little away from her, and then turn round, and look back. Then at last the true landscape will become visible. You must have tasted, however briefly, the pure water from beyond the world before you can be distinctly conscious of the hot, salty tang of Nature's current. (*Miracles*)

Here we have the key to what Lewis (and the other Inklings, and all the Romantics, dating back to S. T. Coleridge) believed about literature. All created things are icons, in some form or another, of spiritual reality. This has sometimes been called "logos epistemology." It's the belief that the creative *logos*, the Word, is within and behind all creation, and all creation points back to it. What we can know is all built on the foundation of the *logos*, to which physical reality points. It's a profound idea that can be expressed as simply as Rich Mullins's words, "Everywhere I go, I see You" ("You" being God).

The reason ancient interpreters of Scripture sought allegorical and spiritual readings was not that they wanted to make Scripture mean lots of different things, but that they believed, rightly, that human beings know on four levels: surface, moral, allegorical, and anagogical (or mythical/spiritual). Our culture believes that the only level of these we can know for sure is surface, that which the five senses perceive and which can be proved to be true in a laboratory. Verifiable facts are the only things we can be certain of, modernistic culture says; spiritual knowledge is relegated to the realm of private opinion. This is nominalistic thinking—the idea that physical reality only has surface meaning and nothing beyond it. It is severely limiting and dehumanizing because we are so much more than bare physical fact.

And this is why the fairy tale is so important. It is imbued with magic, with symbols and pointers to a greater reality. I am not saying that all fairy tales accomplish this equally or that a fairy tale cannot carry with it completely wrongheaded ideas about the world. But the genre of fantasy lends itself to sub-created worlds in which symbols of Christ abound—phoenixes, unicorns, white stags, griffins, and countless other Christ symbols are regular parts of great fairy-stories.

This is why planetary symbolism is embedded in C. S. Lewis's *Narnia* septology; we experience the deeper levels of reality while interacting with these symbols, even if we don't understand them. This is why his Ransom trilogy is built on the scaffolding of literary alchemy. We pass through the stages of black (grief/loss), white (purification), and red (eternal life) with Ransom, whether we understand alchemy or not. These are symbolic pointers to the spiritual reality of the world, in story form.

This is not gnosticism; it's not "secret knowledge" which is more important than physical symbols. It is the belief that the physical symbols do indeed picture reality. It's the conscious *logos* within human beings recognizing that same creative *logos* in the created and sub-created worlds.

How does story do its work on us? The same way the Gospel does: by faith. Coleridge wrote of the "willing suspension of disbelief" created by a good story. This is close, but Tolkien didn't quite like the phrase. He preferred to speak of a sub-creation so effective that it enables *literary belief*—a much more active term. When the spell of a good story with a consistent sub-creation is cast upon us, we believe the story as we are reading it. I'm not saying we believe that it factually occurred, but that we experience what Tolkien called "Secondary Belief," the mind's willingness to fully enter the sub-creation. When we do so, we experience the story along with its characters, interact with its themes and symbols, and are potentially influenced and transformed by them.

Fairy tales, then, are hardly mere entertainment, nor are they trivial stories only fit for children. They are, instead, echoes and pointers to the one great fairy tale that tells us of the sudden joyous turn that has entered history and saved us all.

You best start believing in fairy tales, dear reader. You're in one.

ᚱᚻᛙᛐᚻᛐ ᚻ ᛒᚢᛐᚲᚻ ᛁᛘ ᚻ ᛚᛁᛐᛐ ᛐᛘᚻᛘ ᚻᛘ ᚻᛐᛐ ᛁᛘ ᚻ ᛁᛐᚻᚻᛐᛐᚢᛐᚻ

—Gimli (WNI)

THE INTEGRATED IMAGINATION:
FANTASY IN THE REAL WORLD
by Andrew Peterson

THIRSTY

My grandmother asked what kind of books I liked to read.

"Fantasy novels," I said. I probably had a *Dragonlance* book hidden in my backpack, next to the Walkman with the Tesla tape, the *TransWorld Skateboarding* mag, and the Trapper Keeper with a Camaro on the front.

"Isn't that sort of thing for girls?" she asked. She tilted her head back to better see me through her glasses.

"What do you mean? There's nothing girly about them."

"Hmm." She went back to her game of solitaire while I tried to tone down my defensiveness.

"Granny, I'm serious. Lots of my friends read them, and I don't know a single girl who does."

"Well, I guess times have changed," she said with a sad little shake of her head.

We went back and forth for a few minutes before I realized that when I said "fantasy" she thought I meant *romance*, the steamy kind—you know, the paperbacks with the scarlet covers and flowing scripts, always with a ravished woman wrapped in the arms of a blonde dude with breeches and riding boots and no shirt, muscles so big he could snap the ravished woman in half, and from the way she's looking at him it seems she wouldn't mind so much if he did. His name is probably Dirk. No wonder my grandmother looked worried.

"No, Granny," I said with relief. "*Fantasy* novels. Swords and dragons and stuff. The less romance the better." That wasn't strictly true, because in *Dragons of Autumn Twilight,* Tanis Half-Elven and elf princess Lauralanthalasa (I'm not kidding) had a thing going, but they had to keep it quiet because her people mistrusted his half-humanness and it created all kinds of romantic tension, plus the War of the Lance interfered and all. But mostly there were dragons. And dwarves. And magic weapons and dungeons and taverns teeming with thieves and adventurers.

I remember Christmas morning 1987 when I tore the wrapping paper off of several *Dragonlance* books—books that I swore to my dad weren't the same as *Dungeons & Dragons* games, though it turned out they were. Almost exactly the same, in fact, but in book form. Even more startling, I didn't turn into a devil-worshipping delinquent, nor did the books spontaneously combust on the holy ground of the church parsonage. On the contrary, I'm almost forty now and I still remember the warm tingle in my fingers when I first held those pulp paperbacks. I can still smell them. If I close my eyes I can see the cover painting by a guy named Larry Elmore. It featured the aforementioned Tanis Half-elven, Caramon the warrior, Goldmoon the barbarian princess, Flint the dwarf, and Tasslehoff the kender standing in an autumnal vale with a red dragon coiled behind them. The whole gang was looking at the camera, so to speak, as if waiting for me to step into the book and join them. Now it all seems so cliché, but at the time I didn't know and didn't care.

Each chapter of those books opened with an illustration of something which, to an eighth grade boy, was awesome. I filled notebooks with drawings of those dragons, talismans, old stone doorways, and walking lizards called *Draconians*.[1] I thought about those stories in class, and read them after I failed tests, and talked about them with my brother and our nerdy friends while we built skateboard ramps

---

[1] I'm aware, of course, that the villainous Draconians are suspiciously similar to the Fangs of Dang in *The Wingfeather Saga*. I'm also aware that the fall of a certain dog in *North! Or Be Eaten* echoes the fall of a certain wizard in the Mines of Moria.

in the garage. The books lifted me straight out of the mossy pines of North Florida and plopped me down in a magical world, just as surely as Lucy stepped through the wardrobe and found herself in Narnia. My young mind crackled with longing, though I wouldn't have known to call it that. I merely said to myself, "Man, that's so *cool*," in an awestruck whisper.

Not long after that, at my older brother's behest, I read David Eddings's *The Belgariad*, a five-book epic fantasy about a kid named Garion who eventually learns to speak a secret spy language with tiny movements of his fingers. If that weren't cool enough, he also saves the world by recovering an orb. I wonder how many times an imaginary world has been saved by the recovery or destruction of a magic item? I loved these books almost as much as I loved the *Dragonlance Chronicles*, partly because it seemed like I read the whole thing in about five minutes. I don't know how Eddings did it, but you can *burn* through those books. Around the same time I read Stephen King's *It* and *The Talisman* (which he wrote with Peter Straub), both of which ought to be considered fantasy novels, and neither of which are as good as I remember them.

My brother also got me hooked on David Gerrold's *The War Against the Chttor* series, which launched me over to the somewhat parallel genre of science fiction.[2] The *Chttor* books raised the bar and lowered it at the same time. Gerrold is, as they said in my neck of the woods, one smart dude. He used the *Chttor* books not just to tell a story with the usual spaceships but also to philosophize, which is one of the best things about sci-fi. The books explore everything from war tactics to ethics to religion to sexuality—but to my relief, there were also plenty of guns, zombies, and wormy critters that wanted to eat the world. I felt my mind expand a little while I was reading them, but it also sank a few notches into the gutter; from time to time even my hormonally-charged high-school self felt a little icky after reading them. Even so, there were moments of bliss when I closed my door at night, switched on the reading light, cracked open the paperback of *A Rage for Revenge,* and could almost hear the hiss of the pressurization system kicking on as I stepped onto the

---

[2] Gerrold's biggest claim to fame is that he wrote the memorable Star Trek episode "The Trouble With Tribbles."

space transport. Gone were the humid bedsheets and the oscillating fan and the mossy trees of Florida, gone was my nascent fear that I would be miserable for the rest of my life, gone were my failures; I was saving the world, baby, and I might not make it back alive.

Then I'd wake on the ugly green couch in my room to the sound of my dad stomping through the house singing "Rise and shine, give God the glory-glory" in full preacher voice. It was time to embark on another day of school, another day of facing what felt like an enormous waste of time—except for those few minutes between failures when I could duck through the trapdoor of my book and emerge into a world of real beauty and real danger, which meant real heroism and the possibility of real purpose. I was hungry for it. Maybe even starving.

Every time we drove the thirty minutes to Gainesville, the nearest town with a mall, I headed straight for Waldenbooks. When I got to Waldenbooks I headed straight for the fantasy/sci-fi section, which at the time boasted only a few shelves. Always with a tantalizing fraction of that same tingle I felt on Christmas morning in 1987, I ran my fingers over the spines of all those paperbacks: Anne McCaffrey's *The Dragonriders of Pern*, Ursula K. LeGuin's *Earthsea Chronicles*, Lloyd Alexander's *Prydain Chronicles*, an ever-increasing number of *Dragonlance* books (now there are about two hundred), the *D&D* spinoff *Forgotten Realms* (which I never cared for, though the covers were killer), Stephen R. Lawhead's *The Pendragon Cycle,* Robert Jordan's *The Eye of the World*, Terry Brooks's *The Sword of Shannara*, and of course, towering above them all, J.R.R. Tolkien's *The Lord of the Rings*—a book I hadn't read, which caused my brother no end of consternation. I had seen the animated films seven hundred times, so I didn't think I needed to read it yet. (Don't be angry. Tolkien, for me, came later.) But hobbits aside, I stood in the aisle at Waldenbooks and *yearned*, I tell you. I was drawn to those book covers like a deer to a salt lick, and like a salt lick they only made me thirstier. I couldn't get enough.

In those days, I was restless without a book in my hands, without the hope of some new story around every turn to enliven my deadening senses. Unlike most of my friends, I didn't want a truck or a job or a scholarship; I wanted a horse and a quest and a buried treasure. But there *were* no real quests anymore. Not in my town.

So I had to make them up. And that led to a series of hijinks that I'll write about when I'm old and most of the witnesses are dead and the statute of limitations has run out.

LONELY

But I left out something significant when I told you about my conversation with Granny Peterson: when she asked me what kind of books I liked to read, the prevailing feeling I remember is bashfulness, just a few inches shy of outright embarrassment. I was standing in her front room with my hand on the table where the grownups always played Canasta, and I stared at the linoleum floor, wishing she hadn't asked me that question. Ask me about something else, I thought. Anything else. Skateboarding or girlfriends or grades or Jesus. Leave my stories alone. My craving for those tales occupied a private part of my adolescence; they represented my loneliness, the only antidote for which was the seemingly impossible dream that life could be lived alongside trusty companions and in defiance of great evil.

I looked out her window and saw crabgrass, old trucks, clouds of mosquitoes, and gravel roads, a rural slowth[3] that drawled, "Here's your life, son. Make do." But my books said, "Here's a sword, lad. Get busy." A persistent fear sizzled in my heart, a fear that there existed no real adventure other than the one on the page, and that I was doomed never to know it. Doomed to a life of failure. There's that word again. I felt called to adventure but saw no way to get there, so instead I read about adventures and kept that dream alive by keeping it to myself. How do you explain that to Granny? How, for that matter, do you explain it to anyone?

That's why, whenever I meet someone who grew up devouring those stories, I have a hunch that I know something about them. Something secret. When I have a conversation with someone about a common love for fantasy stories, there's a

---

[3] You won't find this word, which means "slowness," in the dictionary, but you will find it in more than one book by Walter Wangerin, Jr., thus establishing its provenance and proving its awesomeness.

subtext, in my mind at least: *You were hungry too, weren't you? You thought you were alone, just like I did. You had something to escape from, and these stories were a way out. You may have only said to yourself, "Man, that's cool," but I think I know what you really meant.*

Don't be afraid, dear reader; your secret is safe with me.

But sooner or later, I had to abandon the salt lick. I needed water. Sometime between the onset of adolescence and my diploma, I discovered music, and music was the horse that bore me safely out of town. Music was the call to adventure, however self-serving and reckless that adventure may have been in the beginning. It was also the doorway through which the object of my quest entered my heart.

AWAKE

In the summer of 1993 I was a foundering young man chaperoning at a youth conference called CIY (Christ in Youth), when one morning on a hillside by the chapel, I watched the sun rise on the green mountains. They were softer and more majestic than any landscape I had imagined existing in Krynn or Prydain or even Middle-earth. They were *real* mountains. My CD Walkman was on repeat, and again and again I heard Rich Mullins sing the lines, "I see the morning moving over the hills / I can see the shadows on the western side / and all those illusions that I had / they just vanish in your light."[4] The sun was rising on me, pushing the shadows of my failure and fear farther and farther away until the whole world was bright and peaceful as only an Appalachian dawn can be when you're nineteen and weeping with the surety of true forgiveness and true love. What I was looking for all along had found me instead.

Not once did I suspect in all my sketching and reading and aching to enter the stories I read that Jesus was calling to me through them. Jesus was mostly an idea. There was church, the life I was supposed to long for, and then there was the life I actually longed for. You see, I was the victim of imaginational segregation. On one

---

[4] "Home," from the album *Winds of Heaven/Stuff of Earth*, Rich Mullins (1988)

hand there was my compulsion to be a Christian—a cultural and familial paradigm that I happily ascribed to and had little reason to resist—and on the other hand I nurtured a mostly secret affection for what were, more or less, fairy tales. Looking back, the same was true of my obsession with comic books and films and music. In each of those art forms I encountered a world that seemed more vivid than the one I was in. With comics I saw bold lines and bright colors, heroes with muscles and courage, internal struggles, true evil to confront and to defeat; with music it was driving riffs and sad solos, passionate vocals and otherworldly sounds that gave voice to my indecipherable emotions; with fantasy novels it was mystery and beauty and danger, stirring accounts of sacrifice, comrades in arms, and whole cities suspended in the boughs of old trees. Outside my window was a sleepy southern town, a place I considered unworthy of much consideration; but inside my mind was darkness and beauty, good and evil, music that spoke a language I felt born to speak. The dark and the light, the danger and destiny—all of it was more beautiful than the world I was in.

I wanted to enter that beauty. And I decided the only way to engage it, apart from my imagination, was to create it. I could draw, or play the piano, or write. If I could make something beautiful, maybe I could forget for a few moments how drab I was, how useless I felt, how lonely was this dull and lifeless life I had been given—and that dull life included Christianity as I understood it. I was, of course, projecting my disappointment with myself onto everything else—everything but the world in my mind, built out of song and story and that terrible, secret longing. The grass was oh-so-much greener on the Other Side. The mountains were taller and the water was sweeter and the stories were better, too.

Things were different, though, that morning on the hillside in East Tennessee. Life itself—the one I was living—for once outshone the life I had yearned for. This beautiful, broken world, having hidden in plain sight my whole life, suddenly ambushed me. It had lain in wait for the perfect moment to spring, a moment comprised of many nuances: the perfect song at the perfect hour of the day, the contrition of my hungry heart, the intricate staging of each act of beauty that had led me to that dewy lawn, and the brooding spirit of God draped over the valley like a mist. "Drink," the Spirit told me, "and thirst no more."

I'm not saying this was my actual conversion, but it was a salient moment that perhaps marked the end of a season of struggle. When the shadows cast by my disappointment and self-hatred were banished by the light of the forgiveness, the acceptance, and the infinite affection of Christ, I could see the world around me for the miracle it was. I could see *myself* as a miracle. Scripture teaches that when God looks at a Christian he sees Christ's righteousness[5]—in a similar way, the Christian is now free to see Christ in everything. Even himself. I was gloriously alive, and I was at home in the palm of God's hand.

FEAST

I abandoned fantasy. I had no need for it, so I thought, because the world I was in pulsed with loveliness. I was wide awake to God's presence. I cried when I sang in church. That was a new one for me. The girl I dated was beautiful, and it was no problem for me (or less of a problem, at least) to honor her and my God by resisting the usual teenage temptations. The Bible became fascinating for the first time since I had read Revelation at church camp to see how imminent was the apocalypse in order to gauge my remaining party time. Now I read it because it felt alive. I read it to know the God Rich Mullins seemed to know so well. And you know what? It worked. During the first few weeks of Bible college the story of the Old Testament lit up my imagination with stories of battle, espionage, love triangles, deception, failure, heroism, and the promise of redemption; mine was an imagination well-prepared for the invasion of the Gospel story. The soil had been fertilized in my youth with a hundred tales that had taken root and grown but had born no fruit; those old stories withered, then decayed and composted, readying the ground for the life-giving seeds that were coming.

I feasted on the meat of the Gospel for four years. I don't want to give the impression that I was a perfectly obedient model student, or that I rejoiced in writing

---

[5] "For our sake he made him to be sin who knew no sin, so that in him we might become the righteousness of God" (2 Cor. 5:21 ESV).

papers on the problem of evil or the kings of Judah. In many ways I was still the bonehead I always was. And yet, I no longer felt that awful lack of purpose, which is, I suppose, a lack of hope. Now there were songs to be written. There were concerts to play. I wanted to tell people this story that had changed me, and through the lens of all my newfound hope, the world and every person I met seemed to shimmer with God's presence. I read commentaries, I read every class syllabus, I read the Bible, I read papers. I was eating meat, meat, meat, and more meat.

At the beginning of my senior year, with a bit of leftover student loan money burning a hole in the pocket of my chapel slacks, I accidentally bought *The Chronicles of Narnia* from the college bookstore. I was hunting for the semester's textbooks when I spotted all seven paperbacks in an attractive slipcase, much like the set I grew up with. I stood in the aisle with an unwieldy stack of textbooks and three-ring binders in one hand, while with the other I experienced a familiar tingle in the tips of my fingers as I ran them over the books that contained the magic of Narnia. There was a sudden sensation of clarity in the room, as when someone has been fussing with the television antenna and the static resolves at once into a clean picture. I knew if I moved, I'd lose the station. I remembered the word I heard that morning on the mountain: "Drink."

The books went home with me, and I showed them to Jamie (to whom I'd been married for about a year). "For our future kids," I said, but that wasn't the whole truth. They were for me, too. I had read so much non-fiction in college that I was craving something light and non-required. Somehow, during my last semester of school, even though I was doing a steady stream of concerts and I needed to complete an internship and twenty-two hours of credit to graduate, I managed to read C. S. Lewis's story of Aslan and Narnia for the first time since childhood. I read it all the way from the wardrobe to the last battle.[6] I thought of it as a literary retreat,

---

[6] I maintain that the books should be read in the order in which they were written and published, not chronological order. Lewis mentioned to a child in a letter, in an offhand way it seems to me, that perhaps they'd be best read chronologically, thus publishers have altered the original sequence in subsequent editions. If you disagree, I'm happy to best you in a rasslin' match.

indulging some of my childhood reading tendencies to give my brain a rest from academia. But instead, I experienced something much deeper.

The reintroduction of fairy tales to my redeemed imagination helped me to see the Maker, his Word, and the abounding human (but sometimes Spirit-commandeered) tales as interconnected. It was like holding the intricate crystal of Scripture up to the light, seeing it lovely and complete, then discovering on the sidewalk a spray of refracted colors. The colors aren't Scripture, nor are they the light behind it. Rather, they're an expression of the truth, born of the light beyond, framed by the prism of revelation, and given expression on solid ground. My final days in college were spent studying the books of Ezekiel and James in class, writing song lyrics in the margins of my syllabi, and reading, at last, *The Lord of the Rings*, that exquisite spray of refracted light.

BRIDGE

And now we come to the point. Tolkien's story bears many similarities to those I read in high school (mostly due to their imitation of him), including the lure of escapism. In the same way the *Dragonlance* books had whisked me out of high school, Tolkien's books transported me out of college for a few precious minutes each day. But whether it was because of my own awakening to the beauty of life through the saving truth of the Gospel or because of Tolkien's own faith and attentiveness to the Holy Spirit while writing *The Lord of the Rings*, when his story ended the world around me held more possibility, not less; it was brighter, not duller; my eyes were clearer, not dimmer. Tolkien and Lewis, both in their own way, lifted me out of this world to show me a thundering beauty, and when I read the last sentence and came tumbling back to earth, I could still hear the peal. I hear it to this day.

God allowed the stories to lift the veil on the imaginary world to show me the *real* world behind it—which ended up being, in the end, the one I was already in.[7]

---

[7] This idea of coming full circle is described by G. K. Chesterton in *Orthodoxy*, as well as in this passage from the introduction to *The Everlasting Man*: "There are two ways of getting

The real world, at least in part, isn't out there somewhere, nor is it in my mind, it's *here*, right under my feet. All around me. Tolkien and Lewis held the fabric of Narnia or Middle-earth in one hand and clutched ours in the other, building a bridge across which we could set out for perilous realms and yet return safely with some of the beauty we found there. The ache we feel when we read about Frodo's voyage from the Grey Havens, the ache we feel when Lucy hears the thump of solid wood at the back of the wardrobe is telling us that yes, there's another world. It's a world so beautiful you can hardly see it through your tears. So let Christ dry your eyes, then look around you. The stories that awaken us are meant to awaken us not only to the reality to come but to *this* world and its expectant glory. Too often we retreat into the pages of our longing only to return disconsolate to the kitchen or the classroom—we're escaping *from* and not *to*. But to the happy child who climbs a tree and imagines it a castle turret, the tree is no less lovely. She sees in the forest a universe of possibility, and could clamber there for days; she's as present to the castles in her dreams as to the sweeping limbs from which she swings.

A few years ago I dug out a few of the fantasy novels I adored and found them mostly empty. Not only have my tastes changed (the quality of the writing left something to be desired), but most of the stories strike me as a way to pass the time rather than to enrich it. The accoutrements of fantasy and science fiction still hold their appeal for me; dragons and quests and epic tales are appetizing seasonings, to be sure, but seasonings don't make a meal. I still occasionally read a story for the excitement of it, but a mere quickening of the pulse is a passing pleasure; my tired heart longs to beat stronger and steadier, because the race is long. Sometimes my sustenance, when

---

home; and one of them is to stay there. The other is to walk round the whole world till we come back to the same place; and I tried to trace such a journey in a story I once wrote . . . I conceived it as a romance of those vast valleys with sloping sides . . . It concerned some boy whose farm or cottage stood on such a slope, and who went on his travels to find something, such as the effigy and grave of some giant; and when he was far enough from home he looked back and saw that his own farm and kitchen-garden, shining flat on the hill-side like the colours and quarterings of a shield, were but parts of some such gigantic figure, on which he had always lived, but which was too large and too close to be seen."

it comes to the books I read, comes from deeper wells—even if it means I have to work for it by reading classics or novels that take place not in Hogwarts but in Iowa (which I have learned is no less magical).[8] I have been enraptured by stories about moths and watermelon harvesting and bridge building, and by fascinating non-fiction about city planning and hurricanes and explorers of the Amazon.[9] There's so much out there to read that I doubt I would ever again answer my grandmother's question with: "Fantasy novels." If someone asked me today, my answer would be "Good books." The same is true of music: "Good music." Is that a genre?

That doesn't mean I don't have a soft spot for all those old stories, and when I meet someone who spent the 1980s with his nose in a fantasy paperback, I enjoy the ensuing conversation. I believe the Lord used those books to pique my desire for another world, to exercise the muscle of imagination (if not of prose), and even to comfort a lonely kid. I'm sure God's doing the same for kids all over the country, even now.

I'm not ashamed to admit that when I go to Barnes & Noble I still visit the fantasy section first. I still run my fingers along the spines and study the cover art. And you know what? I still feel that 1987 tingle. Sometimes I even read some of those books. I tell myself it's just for fun, but I'll tell you a secret: I'm on the hunt. Somewhere out there, there's another Tolkien. Somewhere out there, men and women with redeemed, integrated imaginations are sitting down to spin a tale that awakens, a tale that leaves its readers with a longing that hurts just enough to tell them they're truly alive, a tale whose fictional beauty begets beauty in the present world and heralds the world to come. Someone out there is building a bridge so we can slip across to elf-land and smuggle back some of its light into this present darkness.

I'm always looking for that bridge.

If you wanted to, I suppose you could call it a quest.

---

[8] *Gilead* by Marilynne Robinson

[9] In the order mentioned: *Pilgrim at Tinker Creek* by Annie Dillard; *Fidelity* by Wendell Berry; *Winter's Tale* by Mark Helprin; *A Place of My Own* by Michael Pollan; *Isaac's Storm* by Erik Larsen; *The Lost City of Z* by David Grann

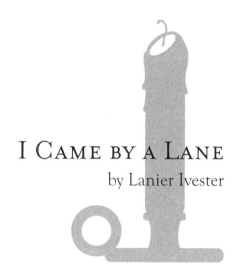

I Came by a Lane
by Lanier Ivester

I came by a lane chestnut-bowered, holly-crowned,
ivy-dressed. The ferns tangle rank with summer-spent flowers
by the wayside, and in the oaks the wood dove sighs,
then sobs, then sighs again.

Under orchard boughs, ewes, sated with windfall, drowse
with one wary eye upon my progress, while their lambs,
looking up from the long, fragrant grass,
mount higher the hill beneath the leaning trees,
distrusting my proximity.

Two rusted gates to close behind with diligent care.
One more flung wide in welcome at the mouth of an
emptied field, and a hill sloping, it seems,
to heaven itself.

I enter, uncertain of such largess, but bold
in this brooding love that marks my passage with unfaltering gift.

Goodness and mercy—twin fruits of a single tree—
I know them well, and on these green hills
most poignantly. Sweeter than the cider-crisp apple
I plucked on my way, and the blackberries crowding the hedges,
and all the dew-kissed sun-ripened nectar of bud
and flower since the world began.

At the crest I pause and look back upon the way I have come,
the swale bent green beneath my boots, and all the more
fragrant for brokenness. The slopes fall away at my feet,
undulating in a gentle descent, only to
rise and crest on neighboring heights, breaking in a spray
of dark trees and hedges, or rolling out in velvet swells.

England is a land of unlikely companions;
Domesticity and Wilderness have met together;
Feral and Tame have kissed each other. And, as it
must always seem to those who love her, Heaven has smiled
His beneficence upon the match.

I stake my claim with a blanket and settle
in a fold of the hedges, bright behind me with bee-life
and breezes and jeweled with autumn's fruit—blue, bloomy sloes,
and crimson hawthorns, and rose-hips flaming a welcome to the birds.

Surely this is what I came for—over sea and land,
and down (and up) those impossible Dorset lanes,
so narrow the hedgerows reach in at the open car
windows as if to protest all the noise and speed
along their quiet ways.

This day, this sweet green turf on which I rest, flinging
my boots aside with the intent of long contemplation.
This robin singing overhead and those rooks settling
a domestic dispute in the dell and the
occasional metallic cluck of a pheasant
surprised into absurdity in a nearby field.

This blue English sky springing cloudless above me
and these English hills spread out like a treasured hoard,
a feast of beauty on which my lean soul grows sleek again
and the child inside me remembers its name.

These things I've known of old, familiar by love's long
association. Before I came here my soul had flown ahead
in years of impatient dreaming, so that when I
did come at last, wide-eyed and breathless,
I was no stranger.

I know what to expect now: those tight endearing lanes
and the high freedom of footpaths with a pub by the
way. I know how the wet grass feels beneath my shod
feet and the stiff sweetness of the air—
though it surprises me yet.

To the south, just over those last blue hills, a green
sea roils and foams on a pebbled shore, and golden
cliffs startle up from its reach, ranking their might to
the east and west before vanishing into mists of faerie.
They are still there, though I can't see them, even from
such a high, holy place. Just so, when I am home,

with my chestnuts and oyster shells ranged in the windowsill,
I still believe in England.

I used to wonder if it were seemly for one
heart to reside in two places at once, to pine
for the one while enjoying the comforts of the other.
But on this green hill my soul is entirely at home,
every fragment gathered together and every
fevered city's fret lulled into stillness, and I know—
it is the most natural thing in the world.

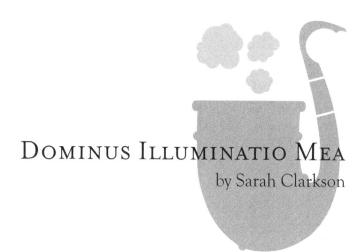

DOMINUS ILLUMINATIO MEA
by Sarah Clarkson

U p slants the light from the river, a pounding of brightness on my closed eyes. From the seat I've stolen for an instant on the grassy bank, I feel motion in the warmth: the swift ebb of storm in a spring sky, the rush of the river to catch the clouds. The shadows of the lithe-armed trees sway over the towpath, and the dark scent of wood smoke rises from the nearby houseboat. I ease my eyes open to peer across the farmer's greening fields. And I exult. For a moment I know the fierce delight the earth takes in its own existence. Joy, that brush of the spirit with something eternal, comes just for an instant to my heart.

But the hot stab of remembrance prods me to my feet and shatters my instant of transcendence. A different joy dawns, for I have an essay due today. The bookish bustle of Oxford draws me, and I do not resist, for that other world, the world of books, is also my love, and I live in my flat beside the river precisely because I am a student, joined for a time to the legions of scholars burrowed in the venerable Oxford libraries. The sacred hush of study awaits me, the pleasure of teetering piles of books on my desk and countless other volumes close at hand. Here, I may delve as deeply into the world's knowledge as zeal and curiosity will take me, for the book I need, the answer I want, is always at my fingertips. Here, all quests for enlightenment may be outlined and ordered by the scholar's alchemy; this is the skill that I have come to Oxford to learn.

Yet, as I rise I laugh, a rueful, curious laugh. My life here is a strange mixing of worlds, one of words and wisdom sought within stone walls, and the other of this river space of wild beauty that will not be caught in the net of mere language yet speaks to my heart as clearly as the voice of a friend. Which will I choose? Sometimes I feel that there is an impossible divide between the scholar who works to know what is sure and the dreamer who knows what is voiceless but true. I hunger to understand what beauty communicates and how it may be set against all that is known by the stricter articulation of logic and reason. In a way, I have come to Oxford to reconcile the scholar and the artist, to bring these twin voices within myself into harmony, so that I may speak forth the silent meaning I find in every experience of beauty.

C.S. Lewis, who walked these same towpaths and haunted these same libraries, understood the tension I feel. It was, in fact, the tension of beauty in a hard pull against the truth of mere reason that prompted his journey to faith. *Surprised by Joy*, his spiritual autobiography, is the subject of my research this week. In this memoir, Lewis states that he had almost to tell two stories, so keen was his sense of division between what he knew by experience—the great "Joy" found in and through nature, story, music, and myth—and the outer, factual life, ordered by reason and, to him at that time, the only provable reality. For Lewis it was a constant and nearly unbearable dichotomy. Could the inner Joy he knew be as real as the world he could touch and see?

I ask the same question of myself as I leave the river walk and join the flow of students up George Street. With the day's first raindrops in a patter on the cobblestones, I duck down a side alley, hugging the stone walls and their spindly ivy, glancing into the covered market and sniffing the fresh fruit before I hurry on my way toward the famous Radcliffe Camera. Having shown my library card shown to the solemn-faced guard, I take the wide stone steps by twos in my hurry to start the day.

Ensconced, finally, at a desk by the window, I hold my breath against the cough that wants to come. The bright air of the library and the walls vaulting from stone pillar to domed ceiling make the sneeze of a mouse sound like a trumpet in here. But this is my favorite place to work. This great circular room, the upper storey of the iconic Oxford Camera, has a sea-like quality of light that plays on the pale green walls and white dome and glimmers amidst the cave-like nooks of the book-laden shelves. Thomas Bodley himself, the library's founder, raises his stone eyebrow at all of us from his statue's perch over the doorway. The desks stretch out from the center of the room in lines, like spokes from a wheel, each shabby wooden cubicle smoothed from the use of many students.

Someone braver than I has coughed across the room, and it frees me to stir a bit myself. I settle as deeply into my angular chair as I can, set my papers at comfortable slants, and turn first to my battered copy of *Surprised by Joy*. I am swiftly immersed, for this chapter describes just what I am hungry to understand: the different ways we know what is true. Haunted by Joy but bound in obedience to Reason, Lewis describes his relief at finding philosopher Samuel Alexander's identification of two kinds of knowledge: Contemplation and Enjoyment.

Contemplation was the knowledge that Lewis had by training—the skilled, ruthless deconstruction of every object and thought for the study of its parts. Contemplation is the knowledge of observation and analysis, the scholar's knowl-edge, the scientist's scrutiny, the Oxford-and-books study in which I am engaged. Lewis created his own picture of this by describing a man standing in a darkened tool shed with a beam of light slipping in over the door. The view to be had by looking *at* the beam he equated with Contemplative knowledge. Psychologists, sociolo-gists, and anthropologists, he listed as those who look at a thing by Contemplation, standing apart from the experience they observe.

I glance up from my reading, aware of a rapid dimming in the sea-like light. Shadows flock through the windows, thick with the navy tinge of a storm that broods outside. Darkness seeps through the wide air of the room, and I notice the sudden glow of the lamps at each desk as they gleam out on the balconies above me like small, unblinking stars. The first drops of rain tap the windows with restless fin-gers, then gather to a rush over the domed roof, sounding like a thousand whispers spoken at once. With the voice of the rain in my ears, with shadows at my elbows,

I sit at the heart of the storm and turn again to my book to read what it means to know by Enjoyment.

This is the knowledge of experience. It was the mystics and lovers, Lewis said, whose perception of faith or romance came through what they touched, tasted, and felt. We know love not by observing it in another but by being within it ourselves. Grief is an ache in our belly, not a thought to be calmly studied. Using the tool shed idea again, Lewis described Enjoyment as the knowledge gained by those who step into the sunbeam, entering the light, experiencing not only the warm glow of the sun itself, but seeing along it into the green summer world outside.

Lewis knew the Joy he describes in *Surprised* from within its aching beauty. To stand apart from the thrill of "northerness" that he knew in his reading of Norse legend and try to analyze it would be to abandon or even to destroy the experience he found in the story. The knowledge of enjoyment, Lewis wrote, comes in the pain of a wounded man, the transported joy of the lover, the ecstasy of the pagan dancing to his gods. I think of the Joy I knew on the river. Did I touch Reality in that instant?, Did I encounter some facet of God?

I close the book and look at my watch. The pace of my heart quickens, for I have only an hour left to finish my essay. I set to the job amidst the rustle of other flustered students, the tap of fingers on keys, and the light thickening with after-storm gold out the window.

It is 3:15 now, and a race down busy George Street and up the cobbles outside of St. Peter's College has brought me to the hushed, book-lined, light-filled confines of my tutor's rooms just in time. I sink with quickened breath and flushed face into a green armchair and glance up at three paintings of scenes from the works of Lewis. One shows a giant god of a man instructing a small mortal. I feel this to be an appropriate image as I turn to read my paper aloud to a tutor who has read all of C.S. Lewis's books more times than I care to know. He nods from his corner by the window, and I begin with as steady a voice as I can muster. He turns when I am finished and the room fills with silence.

"So, what questions did you find?"

For a second, I am silent, wondering if I should describe the dichotomy I've personally known between my experience of beauty and the scholarly work I do here. I take the plunge, wondering aloud how my experience of God's reality in beauty, however exultant, can ever stand next to logic and analysis and be held the truer.

My tutor keeps his place by the window as he listens, wrapped in a woolen coat warm enough for a Narnian winter, his eyes on the courtyard below. A beam of low, wintered sunlight falls across his face, obscuring the keen eyes behind his glasses, lending an inscrutable calm to his countenance that brings my rambling words to a halt. Silence falls, the pale light pools on the carpet. He turns to face me, and in a voice of perfect English precision, smoothed and deepened by the evensong chants he performs as college chaplain, he tells me I must not look at beauty that way. Simply must not. The knowledge of experience is a language without words. I can see his eyes now, focused on my face, willing me to understand.

But I am silent, considering the concept of a language of experience. This makes what I know in beauty to be equally valid when set against reason, equally true, but not to be measured against analysis. To help me along, my tutor reminds me of a difficult Lewis essay I read last week on the symbolic nature of language. In a brilliant piece called "Bluspels and Flalansferes," Lewis explained that every word we speak is a metaphor for something beyond itself. Words aren't Truth itself. They are merely symbols pointing back to what is Real. The language of beauty that I encounter in my riverside rambles, or in the music I love, or even in the stories of Lewis himself, is simply another series of symbols. But the silent truth I touch within them is just as valid as words, for beauty gestures constantly back to the Real, to God in his ultimate, eternal loveliness.

At the end of my session, I stride hard for the fields near my flat, determined to pound out all the adrenaline stored by study, all the questions provoked by what I've read. I reach Port Meadow, the ancient grazing lands adjoining the city of Oxford. These flood plains are ever green in their undulation toward the Thames, unchanging with the cold of winter or heat of summer. I reach them just as the sun gets level with the tops of the trees. The air is icy and the trees black against the last, honeyed light. I tromp through the rutted grass with the cord of the river frayed by three duck ripples on my left.

I halt at a point where I can watch the sun seem to settle on the arrow tip of an old fir. The low-day gleam of it is a great eye fixed upon me. I lift my face to meet it, and am still. A great flock of birds, many hundreds strong, wheels suddenly around me, high in the fragile blue of the sky, and I feel myself fixed in the center of God's sight while his Spirit flutters through me.

In that instant, I understand what my tutor meant. The earth itself is a language without words. These ancient fields, that unbending tree, the sun like the eye of God—they each figure forth, *mean* God to us who dwell within his earth. Their voices, as the Psalmist says, have gone out through all the earth, and he does not mean this figuratively. We walk as ceaseless students in the knowledge of experience, our very existence an immersion in the meaning, communicating world in which God has placed us.

"The whole universe is, in the last resort, mental," Lewis finally recognized in *Surprised by Joy*. "Our logic is participation in a cosmic *Logos*." In this realization, he began to reconcile the long-standing divide between beauty and truth, joy and study, words and the silent language of his spiritual Joy. I begin to feel that it is possible for me as well.

Night has come to Oxford now as I hurry down Broad Street with a group of friends. Trinity, my own college, settles itself in for the night as we trundle past its huge iron gate. We have just left Evensong at New College, and our minds are still filled with the chant of the choir boys and the images of candlelight flung through a medieval chapel gemmed with stained glass, of the walls of stone saints, and of the dark wooden roof carved with giant angels. Our street is only dimly lit; the walls of the colleges arch up on either side of our way, golden stone and shadow making an eerie maze of the street. We whisper as we scurry toward warmth and cider at the pub, for though we all agree on the beauty of the place and words we have just left, we do not agree on what they mean.

Beauty moves us to desire the ideal in ourselves and in the world we inhabit. This we all concede. But we differ on what it means to seek the ideal. One friend suggests that the desire for goodness is simply another facet of evolution. The beauty in the chapel moves us, and of course, he says, we want to become a purer self. But in his view, God need not be the cause of the beauty nor the end of our quest for perfection.

Before I can reply, we reach the door of the pub and are plunged into a roiling sea of people. With laughter cresting and crashing around us, we jostle our way upstairs and snatch any unused chairs we can find so that the six of us can finally sit. Two of the boys go in search of drinks as the rest of us hold down the fort, leaning close over the rickety wooden tables to finish our debate.

"But what," I have to nearly yell at my friend, "is the point of evolution? What are we evolving toward?"

Even as the words leave my lips, I remember something Lewis had said. In describing himself before faith, Lewis spoke of his thinking as centrifugal, centered upon his own existence, his own assumed power to control both the transcendent Joy he loved to feel and the rational explanation of it. But Joy, the stab of beauty, the strike of wonder, left him always with desire, as if it were the burning touch of some great Person beyond, of which the music or book or landscape had been but a messenger.

Joy, Lewis realized, points always back to the Reality from which it comes. With that understanding, he began the centripetal movement to belief in a Mind beyond his own. Lewis's consequent conversion to Christianity was a completion of this movement. He recognized that Joy causes us to "yearn, rightly, for that unity which we can never reach except by ceasing to be the separate phenomenal beings called 'we.'" Lewis assented to the fact that his knowledge was dependent on another's, and with that assent, he believed in God.

Even as I debate with my friend, the thought of this whirls in my mind. If the whole world comes to me from the mind of God, then nothing I encounter, logic or loveliness, word or wordless joy, has meaning apart from him. Each is simply one more symbol figuring forth the real truth of his being. I don't think I convince my friend, but I begin to understand in my own right, and for tonight, that is enough.

When midnight looms heavy and close, we force our way out of the crowd. The still, star-brightened air is grace on our skin after the strife of the crowded pub. We stroll down the street, our words spent, our eyes turned up to the church towers and odd-shaped buildings hunkered across the skyline. Outside of the history faculty we stop amidst a jumble of bicycles and wait for those who need to unlock theirs for the short trip home. My eyes wander up the walls of the stately old building and are caught by a carved inscription near the roof on the left-hand side.

"Dominus Illuminatio Mea." I halt, frozen by those words. I have seen them carven on buildings all over Oxford—over doorways, beside statues, framed in ivy—as if the walls themselves speak forth the ancient motto of Oxford: "The Lord is my Light," or more literally, "The Lord is my Illumination." And in one swift rush amidst the chill and starlight, I truly understand.

I see that throughout its many centuries of scholars, the wisest in Oxford have been those who understood, as Lewis did, that in every facet of our life and experience, in every nook of the world, in every last depth of study, in every sentence of a book, God reaches out to our minds, our souls, our beings. God illumines me through the crisp, marching order of words that speak his logical truth but also through the taste and touch of the earth, the dim nights and bright mornings, the dusky enchantment of music, the force of love given and received, and again through the words in which I cup these experiences. One in the other, the *knowing of mind* taking hands with the *knowing of heart*, each flowing in and out of the other, but always expressing the one, great fact of God. There is no division, for every word and wonder in the universe means and speaks God's love and presence in the life of the world.

Lewis knew this. His faith in God was founded on his acceptance of the fact that life is ultimately something we may only enjoy from inside of experience. God is the one who speaks us into being and sets us in the midst of a world of metaphors that speak forth his goodness and point ceaselessly back to their Creator. We cannot stand apart from our own being and analyze our existence. We can only experience the world and the words given to us by a Mind greater than our own. To believe in God is to know ourselves readers in a vast realm of metaphor. Every touch of truth, goodness, or beauty is one more facet of God's ceaseless communication.

In knowing this, Lewis reconciled his divided thought. Beauty and truth, logic and joy—they all came from the same great Life beating at the core of existence.

This newly unified mind was the foundation from which he went on to create his great works of Christian apologetics, his essays, and his novels for adults and children alike. In the vivid imagery of story and the well-mapped logic of apologetics, he communicated the Reality he had come to know. His imagination and logic were united to body forth the Joy that was the cause and goal of both.

The scratch of a bicycle wheel jolts me back to the present. The world moves again, my friends wheel their bicycles down the deserted streets, and I follow. Peace thrums through my bones and soul as I amble home, for like the heart of Lewis, my own heart is finally unified. Today, I have learned what it means to be a knower and teller of truth in every glory and guise.

We reach the towpath, and through the trees I hear the low hum of the river in its midnight ramble. I am back in my wild world, but I no longer feel the tension of divide. Books and beauty, libraries and riversides, all are part of God's ceaseless illumination. I turn up the gravel path to my door, and Joy is in my soul.

"It is a far, far better book to read than I have ever read. A far, far better book I hold than I have ever known."

—SYDNEY CARTON, Headless Lawyer (WNI)

THE WIND AND THE TREES
by G. K. Chesterton

I am sitting under tall trees, with a great wind boiling like surf about the tops of them, so that their living load of leaves rocks and roars in something that is at once exultation and agony. I feel, in fact, as if I were actually sitting at the bottom of the sea among mere anchors and ropes, while over my head and over the green twilight of water sounded the everlasting rush of waves and the toil and crash and shipwreck of tremendous ships. The wind tugs at the trees as if it might pluck them root and all out of the earth like tufts of grass. Or, to try yet another desperate figure of speech for this unspeakable energy, the trees are straining and tearing and lashing as if they were a tribe of dragons each tied by the tail.

As I look at these top-heavy giants tortured by an invisible and violent witch-craft, a phrase comes back into my mind. I remember a little boy of my acquaintance who was once walking in Battersea Park under just such torn skies and tossing trees. He did not like the wind at all; it blew in his face too much; it made him shut his eyes; and it blew off his hat, of which he was very proud. He was, as far as I remember, about four. After complaining repeatedly of the atmospheric unrest, he said at last to his mother, "Well, why don't you take away the trees, and then it wouldn't wind."

Nothing could be more intelligent or natural than this mistake. Any one looking for the first time at the trees might fancy that they were indeed vast and titanic fans, which by their mere waving agitated the air around them for miles. Nothing, I say, could be more human and excusable than the belief that it is the trees which make the wind. Indeed, the belief is so human and excusable that it is, as a matter of fact, the belief of about ninety-nine out of a hundred of the philosophers, reformers, sociologists, and politicians of the great age in which we live. My small friend was, in fact, very like the principal modern thinkers; only much nicer.

In the little apologue or parable which he has thus the honour of inventing, the trees stand for all visible things and the wind for the invisible. The wind is the spirit which bloweth where it listeth; the trees are the material things of the world which are blown where the spirit lists. The wind is philosophy, religion, revolution; the trees are cities and civilisations. We only know that there is a wind because the trees on some distant hill suddenly go mad. We only know that there is a real revolution because all the chimney-pots go mad on the whole skyline of the city.

Just as the ragged outline of a tree grows suddenly more ragged and rises into fantastic crests or tattered tails, so the human city rises under the wind of the spirit into toppling temples or sudden spires. No man has ever seen a revolution. Mobs pouring through the palaces, blood pouring down the gutters, the guillotine lifted higher than the throne, a prison in ruins, a people in arms--these things are not revolution, but the results of revolution.

You cannot see a wind; you can only see that there is a wind. So, also, you cannot see a revolution; you can only see that there is a revolution. And there never has been in the history of the world a real revolution, brutally active and decisive, which was not preceded by unrest and new dogma in the reign of invisible things. All revolutions began by being abstract. Most revolutions began by being quite pedantically abstract.

The wind is up above the world before a twig on the tree has moved. So there must always be a battle in the sky before there is a battle on the earth. Since it is lawful to pray for the coming of the kingdom, it is lawful also to pray for the coming of the revolution that shall restore the kingdom. It is lawful to hope to hear the wind of Heaven in the trees. It is lawful to pray "Thine anger come on earth as it is in Heaven."

The great human dogma, then, is that the wind moves the trees. The great human heresy is that the trees move the wind. When people begin to say that the material circumstances have alone created the moral circumstances, then they have prevented all possibility of serious change. For if my circumstances have made me wholly stupid, how can I be certain even that I am right in altering those circumstances?

The man who represents all thought as an accident of environment is simply smashing and discrediting all his own thoughts—including that one. To treat the human mind as having an ultimate authority is necessary to any kind of thinking, even free thinking. And nothing will ever be reformed in this age or country unless we realise that the moral fact comes first.

I get up from under the trees, for the wind and the slight rain have ceased. The trees stand up like golden pillars in a clear sunlight. The tossing of the trees and the blowing of the wind have ceased simultaneously. So I suppose there are still modern philosophers who will maintain that the trees make the wind.

Excerpts taken from "The Wind and the Trees," originally published in Tremendous Trifles *(1909)*

"To the last page, I grapple with thee."

—AHAB, Tyrannical Captain, *Pequod* (WNI)

IN THE YEAR OF JUBILATION
(FROM THE BOOK OF FOUND VERSE)
by A. S. Peterson

I generally scoff at New Year's resolutions, which is, perhaps, ironic since a resolution was the impetus for my first novel. But books notwithstanding, I resolve as rarely as possible. Last year, however, I failed completely in my resolute irresolution; I committed to writing a poem a day. It was one of those seemingly manageable writing exercises that quickly became both exhilarating and humiliating. It must be admitted that this resolve served as the engine for a great volume of bad poetry. But even bad writing is worth the trouble. It keeps the muscles in shape.

It was also the year that I first encountered Josh Ritter's music. *So Runs the World Away* caught my attention and held it. I couldn't get enough. And that album led me through the rest of the back catalog, where I discovered other gems like *The Animal Years* and *Hello Starling*. Ritter's lyrics are full of depth and beauty and, most importantly, questions. He plays with big ideas and does so in ways that let them sneak in under your radar; they hang around and throw punches, begging you to get in the ring and wrestle with them. His songs do what good songs should do: they make you think.

Of all his songs, one of my favorites is called "Lantern." It's an earworm—easy to listen to, easy to sing along with, great lyrics. But while the lyrics might feel light at first, they aren't; they demand to be grappled with. In the song, Ritter's claiming that it's a hard, dark world out there, and the only lights we find are each other. "If there's a book of jubilations, we'll have to write it for ourselves," he sings. I thought about that for a while, and then I decided to get in the ring and fight back.

Setting aside the fact that the world is filled with nearly two thousand years of jubilant hymns, paintings, poetry, sculpture, architecture, and every other form of art with which men give thanks and praise, I took up Ritter's challenge. I resolved that each Sunday when I sat down to write my daily poem, I'd write a "jubilation."

By the end of the year, I'd done a pretty solid job of failing my New Year's resolution, but I did eke out well over a hundred poems, about twenty of them Sunday jubilations. I put them away for a while and came back to them this year to see if there was anything useful amidst the chaff. When I read over the jubilations, I was surprised to find that they shared common threads of narrative and imagery. I've culled the worst, and those that remain I've ordered, refined, and edited into the fourteen-poem cycle that follows. Together they are my answer to Ritter's charge that the light in the world has gone out and it's up to men to provide illumination of their own. Keep the music coming, Josh, and thanks for the great song. But along with a great host of other witnesses, I contend otherwise.

So throw away those lamentations
We both know them all too well
If there's a book of jubilations
We'll have to write it for ourselves
—Josh Ritter, "Lantern"

The light shines in the darkness, and the darkness has not overcome it.
—John 1:5 (ESV)

⸺ Invocation ⸺

Rejoice, O dark and formless deep
The light-tongued dawn in his womb awakes
A kingdom is coming nigh

Elements ready themselves for the matter
While Time, the fawn, springs forth to run
Over crackling gases alive in the heat
And groan of star-fires breaching

From the living bedrock,
Whereon Nature's brook runs babbling,
You plucked the perfect stone:
Rounded yet inviolate,
Hewn yet undivided,
Bright by Word within.

Hallowed, it settled into
The palm of your open hand.
You rolled it in your fingers,
Took pleasure in its gleaming
And its great unlooked-for weight.

Then, smiling, you raised it once
To touch with your blessed lips,
And you cast it, hurled it, flaming
Across the starry arch,
Where, descending far, it plunged
Into pools of temporal fullness—
Appearing merely a pebble fallen,
Until out of its plashy drop
A widening diadem rolled.

Over years it rolls,
Even thousands since,
And we bathe in the rising tide
That deepens and ripples,
In billows wide,
Lapping on unhidden stones
In the font of Abraham's longing.

In the early sun, I awaken.
My city awakens beside me.
I stand in a line.
I shuffle forward.
Before me a saint,
Behind me another.
We gather, washed up
Like deadened wood
At the foot of a wizened oak.
We kneel at a table.
We strip off our rags.
We wrestle down
Into stillness and quiet
To take hold of the loaf,
Of the broken loaf,
To water our roots
In sanguine wine.
I rise. I look behind.
A chain of saints
Unbroken stretches
Back to the beginning.
Before me they vanish
In light yet to shine,
Linked by blood, by flesh
Undying, eternal, a memorial
Enacted 'til time and memory
No longer have need
Of these withering rites.

—◦ III ◦—

I have eaten my fill today
I have taken my ease in the sun
Hallelujah

I have traveled without the need
Of a beast in the fertile land
Hallelujah

I turn my wrist and waters rise
I wash, I drink, I cook
Hallelujah

I have, this Sabbath, no trouble to mind
No reason to worry, to fret
Hallelujah

If tomorrow I hunger, thirst, toil
Walk naked the streets alone
Hallelujah
Even so, Hallelujah

Drawn in and deftly limned
By strokes of the penman's script
By line and ligature defined
And dusted upon the page to dry
A mere word of the author's many
A minor part of the play
While the pen swoops on
Through sigil and flourish
A character written, I flatly lie
To wait for the waking hour
When word by Word, in letter raised
I'm enacted boldly and spoken

Make me better, O Lord,
Than I have been
Better tomorrow
Than I am today

We are drifting
Caught in the current
We are fumbling
On the stage in silence
We are hungry
For the gap in the fence
And we turn from
The fertile land

We walk when
We ought to leap
We flee when
You bid us be still
We linger
In the accursed vale
And settle homes
In the hinterland

Make me better, O Lord,
Than I have been
Love me tomorrow
As you have today

I crept in an unlit night
Under an oppressing sky.
A scree of shattered earth
Bit knees and tattered palms.
I huddled low in the black
As it bent upon my shoulder
Like a heel of menace
Grown titan, though wholly empty,
On gobbets of hateful thought.
I writhed beneath it, sniffing,
Searching with ragged fingers,
Raw bones weary to breaking,
Until I found the faultless stone
Within whom hid the Word
Of the world's unstumbled making.
I kissed it, swallowed it whole,
So that it, unhid, within me lives,
Purposes my flesh,
Beats, sings, shines,
Speaks new forms
Upon my trampled body.
It shall, in its time, speak again
The unquiet light,
Unmake the oppressor,
Call to the Lazarine Fields:
"Arise. Arise."

~ VII ~

In the dead of my flesh
I was content to slouch
Away from the light,
Out of the runnel of life.
Dead flesh like mine,
You wore, and are, my cloak.
You breathed my fetid breath.
You loved the vouchsafed stone
Whose weight I hold long-hidden.
Circle over my eyeless life,
Come boldly shout, Illumined Word.
Creation, answer in leap and spiral.
Quicken the hidden stones with words.
Quicken, deepen, dance in fractal.
Quicken and sing me new.

~ VIII ~

The Word has set skies awhirl,
Has lit stars, spun galaxies,
Flung them into void reaches
Where they adorn darkness,
Like lanterns titanic.

The Word is among us,
Within us formed,
Lying ready upon
My humble tongue.

First Command,
Original Expression,
Incarnate Dictum,
Form in my voice yours.
Create the world anew.

~ IX ~

Rose-petal light
Angling down
On heads bowed to
Shuffling feet
The rustle of young ones
Too young to know
Up on tiny knees to see
A parting and gathering
An eddying flow
Saints to the table to kneel
Grace and memory
Comingle, entwine
The whispering priest
The bread of heaven
The body of Christ divine

I give thanks that I am gone.
I rejoice at the flickering Word
Within the husk of flesh I filled
With rotting things and killed.

He found it feeding the entropic worm
And broke Himself in the mending,
To nurture my spark on the blood of starbirth,
To supplant the worm distending.

I'm gone, and now an infant sun
In atomics blooms renewing.
The lanterned skies are unveiled. "Arise."
The earth is following after.
All earth is following after.

The Lord has raised up
The hidden things
And bound them.
The Lord has set them fast
About his uptorn brow.
The Lord has worn sorrows,
And worn them through.
The Lord has hewn gems
From long-sought hearts of coal.
The Lord draws up his raiment:
Bright jewels of the earth,
By thorn and hammer made
Fitting as the lion's mane.
He commands the inviolate stone—
And it sings:

I am in the newly furrowed field.
The earth, fresh-turned,
Is moist between my toes.
The husks of another year's increase
Lie heaped upon the fire.
When their embers cool,
I will spread them over the earth.
Rain shall fall like a bright-tongued ghost.
The sun shall warm the soil.
I am in the rows.
I am in the spaces in between.
My hands hover over the earth,
And I feel explosions whispered.
Life erupts beneath my feet:
Tiny earthquakes, each a rising,
Each a bursting, each a winding promise.
I am waiting patiently.
I am the taker of the harvest.
The promise I have laid in the deep
Breaks, rises, stretches up its infant arms;
It cries out a song sweet to my ears.
I smile. I reply: "Come, O Showers!
Come, Tongues of Light!"
For all the nurture
The broken seed
Will ever seek
Or need,
I am.

~ Benediction ~

The budding trees whisper one to another
Of the season, stirring in sleep, to come
Wherein shall dwell the world again
In the shout of summer's running

Rejoice, O field and barren branch
The deep midwinter of the world has passed
Spring is on the rise

What I Would Now Like to Imagine

by Don Chaffer

I would like to imagine right now—
Sitting on a weathered bench in a flower garden—
That we are all together again
On our way to a symphony in the park.
We have all of our teeth,
Our skin bears no marks of any surgeries,
We have neither lost, nor gained, too much weight.
There are no machines attached to us,
And we are all young.

We will set out our blanket and lawn chairs,
And I will ask if anyone wants to play soccer.
We will all say yes.

We will not be too hungry,
Nor will we have just eaten
And feel light-headed after only a few minutes of play.
We will get thirsty and hot,

And break to drink water,
Dribble it down our shirts, and
Dump it on our heads.

Someone—perhaps Mom—
Will have the idea to take off her shoes and socks
And will walk in the fountain,
Cocking one eye all the while
For someone who might come along and ruin our fun,
    "No dancing in the fountain, please."
But no one comes to say such a thing.

This business with the fountain will break up the game of soccer,
But I will be happy, and I will not be able to
Think of a better reason to break up a good game,

    except perhaps, to get frozen custard at Nick's
    (Nick's will still be in business).

Our laughter will sound,
When it happens, like
A man riding a horse on the other side of a patch of trees:
    Though he is hidden half of the time—
    Now by a clump of leaves,
    Now by a limb,
    Now, a trunk—
    He is riding all the while,
    A thunder of hooves, and flapping cloth.

We will have forgiven one another
So completely, without forgetting offenses,

That to see one another's faces
Will be finally to understand
What love is.

This is how it will be.

"Collicellus talpae est fundamentum cogitationis."
—Prudentius (WNI)

A Night Poem (For Easter)

by Andrew Peterson

I lie in bed these sweet few days
When the windows yet are open
And the weather yet is fine,
And love to hear the dead of night
Announce its living presence
With hoot and croak and creeping vine.

I love the knowledge that for years
As I have waited on the bench
Beneath the juniper tree,
And paid my best attention,
There is an owl I've never seen
An owl, I know, who watches me.

I love the sound of secret things,
I love to hear their nearness,
And to feel their wildness, too.
Three days ago we sowed the seeds

And every hour I checked the dirt
For seedlings pushing through.

I lie in bed awake, alert,
Aware of the God of the Garden.
I sense in the seed a promise,
An unfolding resurrection
In the furrowed row, in soil
And root, in husk and humus.

I sense an ancient heart alive
Who haunts these moonlit acres
Breathing, bringing life from death
Dawn from darkness, song from sorrow.
The night owl swoops, the zephyr sighs,
I hear within the tomb: a breath.

A SEASON'S EATINGS

by Evie Coates

A SPRING-Y VEGETABLE SAUTÉ

*a squeeze of lemon at the end wouldn't hurt either!

Heat two tablespoons <u>fresh butter</u> in large skillet. Saute ½ lb. <u>wild mushrooms</u> of your choosing or foraging -- morels, maitakes, creminis, what have you... for about 4 minutes, over med-high heat. Set aside. To a large saucepan of boiling water, add 1½ lbs. <u>asparagus</u>, diagonally cut into 2-inch bits), 1 lb. <u>sugar snap peas</u>, and 3 bunches <u>scallions</u> (white + light green, cut like the asparagus). Let it roll for about 2 minutes. Drain well, add to mushrooms with 2 more tbsps. butter and a handful of chopped fresh <u>mint</u>, salt + pepper to taste. Eat <u>NOW</u>!

SPRING

BEET AND STRAWBERRY SALAD

Wrap 6 small-medium <u>red beets</u>, scrubbed well, in heavy foil and roast in center of oven for 1-1½ hours at 425°, then unwrap and allow to cool. Peel and cut crosswise into ½" rounds, toss with a bit of <u>red wine vinegar</u>, salt & sugar (one tsp each). Clean and trim about a dozen <u>strawberries</u> and cut similarly, crosswise into rounds. Toss with a lil' squeeze of lemon & a bit of sugar. Arrange these lovely, ruby-hued discs nicely on a plate, crumble some <u>goat cheese</u> over them, and again, with the <u>mint</u>! Tear it into bits and scatter with joy. Add a toss of Maldon sea salt if you have it. Eat and relish.

HEIRLOOM TOMATO AND WATERMELON SALAD

1 4-lb-ish chunk of watermelon, cut into small slabs
3 heirloom tomatoes, sliced (green zebras are super pretty!)
2 scallions, sliced thinly on a diagonal
3 tbsp. chopped fresh dill
½ cup crumbled feta (optional)

Arrange fruits prettily on plate, scatter scallions, dill & feta haphazardly over, dress with a nice glug of good olive oil and a sprinkling of red wine vinegar, kosher salt & fresh pepper.

SUMMER

SOUR CREAM-ROSEWATER ICE CREAM

tart, creamy, aromatic, addictive. the ideal summer sweet with some fresh berries or peaches. Ah! Delight.

1 16-oz. container of sour cream
1½ cups half & half
¾ cup sugar (I also like honey)
2 tsp. fresh lemon juice
1 tsp. rosewater (find at any international foodstore)
⅛ tsp. salt

Whizz all ingredients in a blender (or whisk with much gusto, like I do) and freeze in an ice cream maker. Presto! Deliciousness.

BUTTERNUT SQUASH AND ROASTED RED PEPPER SOUP

In a large, heavy pot over med-high heat, add one large yellow onion, chopped, to 2 tbsps. olive oil. Sauté 'til soft, add 3 garlic cloves, minced. Add 1 2-lb. butternut squash (peeled, seeded, cut into small chunks) and 4 cups chicken broth. Reduce heat, cover, simmer about 45 mins. Let cool slightly, then add 1 cup roasted red peppers (whether from a jar or roasted, coddled, peeled by your own hands) and 1 tbsp. smoked paprika and 1 tsp. each salt + pepper. Puree in batches or use my favorite tool, the immersion blender. Serve with sour cream with lemon zest & salt added. ...warming.

AUTUMN

it's
* autumn
in a dish! *

APPLE CRISP   oven: 375°

about 6 large baking apples, peeled, cored, sliced or chunked-up
½ cup sugar; 1 lemon, juiced; nutmeg
2 tbsp. flour

Toss together, set aside. (and try to avoid snacking on it)

In a bowl, mix: 1½ c. flour, 1½ c. brown sugar, 1 c. oats, ½ tsp. kosher salt, 1 tsp. cinnamon.

Rub in with your fingers: 2 sticks (1 cup) soft butter

Spread over apples in baking dish and bake 45-or-so minutes. Top with ice cream: devour greedily.

OUR FAMILY'S TIME-TESTED, GO-TO, NEVER-FAIL, MOST DELICIOUS... CHILI

YOU MUST SERVE WITH A PLATE OF SOUR PICKLES + CHEDDAR TO BE ADDED AT TABLE

sauté in large, heavy pot 2 cups each of the following, chopped: yellow onion, green pepper, celery. Cook over med- high heat until soft. Add 4 tbsp. chili powder and 2 tsp. ground cumin (maybe a pinch of cinnamon if you're feeling adventurous...)
* Now add 1½ - 2 lbs. ground beef (ground round is what we use), break up with wooden spoon, but not too much -- chunks are marvelous.
* Now add a can of pinto, navy, and light red kidney beans (one of each), a 28-oz. can tomato sauce, and a can of squished up whole canned tomatoes...It's better that way. Let simmer on low for as long as you can stand.

salt + pepper too!

Winter

BEJEWELLED DARK CHOCOLATE BARK

Chop up finely 8 ounces each of good semisweet & good bittersweet chocolate. Put in a glass bowl and microwave (yep!) for 30 seconds. Remove, stir, microwave for another 30. It can be so simple! No double-boiler needed. Hooray! Repeat until just melted. Pour onto parchment-lined sheet tray and spread with rubber spatula. This is the fun part: sprinkle onto surface of chocolate and lightly press into it.......chopped pistachios, golden raisins, dried cranberries, medium-diced dried apricots. The color is dazzling. Then, with a gentle and deft hand, sprinkle with raw sugar, flaked sea salt and... smoked paprika! KILLER

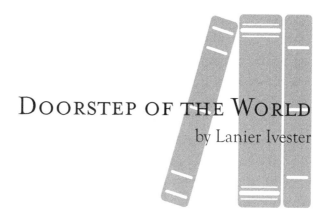

DOORSTEP OF THE WORLD
by Lanier Ivester

On the day Docie Thaxter walked out the back door and cut off across the back east pasture, she hadn't the least idea where she was going. "I'll walk till I'm dead or till I run into something, whichever comes first," she told herself grimly as she stalked through the long, tufted grass that swept nearly to the pocket of her apron. Clelia would be furious that the strawberries were ruined, of course. But for once her sister-in-law's displeasure didn't bother Docie in the least. She was past caring.

The ground was rough with unkempt hillocks and earthen piles of fire ant beds. Her brother Thurman didn't tend this lot as carefully as he did those to the north and west of the house, the ones that could be seen from the road. Those were silken sweeps of luxurious verdure, whereupon the finest, sleekest Black Angus cows in the county feasted like queens and drowsed beneath shade trees in the heat of the day. Their sultan, the sire bull to whom Thurman's grandson had given the name "Black Stuff," was grazing with them, though he was kept up here when his amorous services were not required. Even though she had not the slightest fear of him, Docie wasn't sorry to find the pasture deserted. Black Stuff was as gentle as an old brood mare and never seemed to mind her presence in the least. But if he were here, she would have to say goodbye to him. And that might weaken her resolve.

She paused amid a patch of thistles high on the crest of the eastern hill and looked back down on the farm with a calm, unblinking gaze. Her tired blue eyes, red-rimmed and watery with age, showed no indication of conflict, or of fire. All that had extinguished itself years ago, long before she was old, even. Or perhaps age was her companion from the beginning, reaching its icy fingers back into her childhood, seizing its opportunity to snuff out her hope and the light of her eyes the moment she had given up the fight. Youth had forsaken her, she felt now, in one dark moment of despair. It burned out its brief, mad infatuation and turned its ardor upon others more promising and more gifted. She was abandoned by life itself, and life had been one endless, dreary chore ever since.

She had been old for sixty years; she realized it with a cold shudder. She had grown old at nineteen.

She shaded her eyes with her hand to take in the landscape below. So much was unchanged from her girlhood that she could imagine it was their grandfather's reign and not her equally determined, albeit less good-humored, brother's. Grandpa had been such a droll elf of a man, always on the spy for some bit of mischief or innocent fun. For Grandpa, the long labor of cajoling a living out of the red dirt was a vast and meaningful endeavor, starred with flashes of lightness and goodness and joy like the white-capped sea she saw only once, on a visit to the Gulf as a child. She had stood beside the endless expanse, green and undulating as any of her grandfather's carefully tended fields, flecked with the delicate, rippling curls of foam that kept spending and renewing themselves in every direction. They looked like daisies to her, blooming and fading in rapid succession, gleaming out with friendly glances amid what would otherwise be a terrible immensity. She placed her hand in her grandfather's there on the seashore and felt in the returning squeeze his compassion at her wonder and her bewilderment.

Grandpa had understood things like that, even when she wasn't able to put them into words. He loved the mystery lingering just beyond the fringes of life, embraced it in his inarticulate, homely way with a deference that was as beautiful as any music or poetry in the world. Perhaps more beautiful, Docie thought, as it was so utterly free from self-consciousness: no illusions or hubris to compete with the awe of the thing enjoyed. Such a servant of the mystery her grandfather had been, and it was this deferential hat-tip to the imponderables of the universe that enabled him to look life straight in the eye and laugh. He was the happiest man she had ever known.

Thurman and Clelia had done a good job with the old place. The house and all the outbuildings were well-roofed and in good order, shining like scrubbed faces under fresh coats of whitewash, and the pastures were immaculately kept, uncompromised by weed or wildflower. She stubbed the toe of her Daniel Greens against the rough stalk of the thistle nearest her and turned up a corner of her mouth. Grandpa wouldn't have suffered a thistle a night's lodging, even away up here in the bull lot.

And he would have left the Queen Anne's lace and butterfly weed and daisies of her girlhood in the lower fields. The pastures then looked like meadows, bright with the wings of Painted Ladies and Swallowtails, and Docie used to lie down among them, gazing up at the summer sky with the flutter of life darting above, intoxicated with the actuality of it all. Grandma had lived in a continual terror that she would fall asleep and be trodden on by one of the cows, but Docie never minded them. She said they were too smart for that, at which her grandmother laughed outright and called her crazy as a bessie bug. Grandma had decided and inflexible opinions on things in general and the mental acuity of cows in particular.

Docie actually *had* fallen asleep once, lulled by the wind-whispering grass and the slow, rhythmic munching of the cows nearby, awakening to a bewilderment of intelligent black faces ringed around her with serene curiosity as their massive jaws worked their cud in circular motions. She smiled back up at them and raised herself from the grass without the slightest alarm. All the same, she deemed it wise not to mention the matter to her grandmother.

Even as the memory receded, Docie realized that she had never told anyone about the experience. Such a trifling thing, an inconsequential aside amid the relentless business of life. Only it had made her happy, so happy that her tired heart gave a dull throb at the recollection all these decades later. She had sat there among the cows as an equal, a slip of a girl on level terms with majestic, towering masses of being, and had shared a mutual interest and respect. She had felt their warm, moist breath on her face and heard the impatient stamping of their mighty hooves as they swished their tails against troublesome flies—hooves which Grandma said could crush her in an instant if they'd wanted to. Only they didn't want to, as Docie well understood. She had felt both her aliveness and theirs in the same dizzying instant of recognition, and it tingled through her like an electric current. She had looked them right in the eyes, and they had stared candidly back at her. And there was no fear between them.

How rarely that had been her experience with her human counterparts, she thought, as she turned with a sigh and set her leaden eyes on the scrub thicket of cedars and scrawny pines at the easternmost corner of the hill field. Among those sun-wizened trees there was a sagging gate, rusted fast on its hinges from years of disuse. It had gone so long latched and unvisited that she doubted even Thurman remembered its existence. She might be the only person on earth who either knew or cared that it was there. The thought made her intolerably lonely, like a stranger shivering on the doorstep of the world. But it was very likely. The Cowart place had lain idle for nearly two decades, and the current owners, new these seven years, wouldn't know to look for it.

But Docie knew. Her feet carried her there by instinct. It was both her end and her beginning; she comprehended it with a quiet and dawning certainty. It didn't concern her in the least what lay on the other side. The only thing that mattered was to go through it. If she could once pass that gate, she could leave her life and all its disappointment and secret anguish and devastated hopes behind. Whether she stumbled on, weak but unburdened, or merely sank down into the cool cushion of the grass, never to rise, was of enormous irrelevance to her.

"Till I die or I run into something," she wheezed out, pausing near the top of the hill with her hands on her knees.

It was then that she heard it: children laughing, chiming out from the little copse above like the tinkling of water or song. The sound rippled down the terraces of the hill, washing over her in a light-dappled tide. There was no music on earth like it, nor singing of birds. She closed her eyes and gave herself to the memory, knowing even as she did that the children were all dead or lost or grown old like herself. The music ceased abruptly, and her lids flew open. The lines of her face hardened once more with a marble resolve, but there were tears in her eyes that had not been there before.

They were living somewhere, those lost children—Cassie and Jack Cowart and the others. Perhaps even she herself was among them, alive like a small ghost of herself, laughing at the world and all the things to come. Or perhaps this withered self was the ghost: a ghost upon the earth, restless and mercilessly undead.

Docie sighed. If Clelia had suspected her of such notions she would say that Docie was having one of her spells and hustle her off to bed with the air of an officious martyr, reminding her with every gesture and inflection that she had now not only the work of two for the day, but the inconvenience of an invalid too. Clelia's ministrations were brisk and efficient, like everything else that she did, and utterly, utterly loathsome to Docie. Clelia had a way of making one feel undeserving of her talents, as if the universe had been mismanaged on her account and left greater duties to lesser hands, while her own splashed amid the suds of Docie's forfeited pan of dishwater or flew with flashing needle over the unfinished landscape of Docie's pieced quilt.

"She hates me. She's always hated me." Docie said it aloud as she began picking her way through the grass once more. "And I—," here she paused and drew a sharp breath. If there was one thing that characterized her from her infancy, it was truthfulness. It could be troublesome at times, particularly for other people. Clelia said that she had a morbid conscience. But Docie simply could not bear to misrepresent the facts, no matter the argument. "And I do not love her," she said with calm enunciation through set teeth.

Clelia had been a thorn in Docie's side long before she had married Thurman and taken Docie's place as mistress of the old farm. They were once girls in school together. Clelia had never been one of the laughing little ghosts, however; she had lived in a fine house in town and been the daughter of a prosperous banker. Clelia always looked down on Docie, with a disdain she refused to rumple with the slightest mockery or sarcasm. Her dislike was remote and distant, calculating and superior. And if Clelia had inwardly raged at Docie's consistently higher grades and good standing among the teachers, she never betrayed it by so much as the flicker of an eyelash. She didn't have to: the feeling that hung between them was thicker than words, weightier and more inscrutable, like a poisonous vapor. It had only grown as they had grown older, to Docie's increasing bewilderment and eventual hardening. At first she was mystified by it; childhood rivalries were things people grew out of. But now it was as familiar as her own skin, and just as enveloping. Clelia maintained a general aloofness with all of their neighbors and most of the country folk, but with Docie it was a downright coldness. Strangely enough, the only person Clelia had seemed to hate more than Docie herself was Jack Cowart, and Docie just couldn't fathom how anyone could hate Jack. He had been so nice to Clelia—he had been nice to all the girls. But it had only seemed to make her hate him more.

Docie had given up trying to make sense of it years ago, well before Clelia made up her mind to have Thurman. That was one point on which Docie was never quite comfortable, that Clelia should have set her cap for a farmer when she might have had her pick of the boys in town or at the university. Doubtless, Thurman was a good man, kind and sensible. And he had been quite handsome in his day: he had the look of their mother's people, strong-featured with disconcertingly dark eyes and black hair that stood up in jaunty curls. That hair was all white now, cresting back from Thurman's broad, high brow like a plume of silver-tipped feathers on the helmet of a champion, and his gaze was just as direct as it had always been, though perhaps a trifle sad. Clelia had wanted him, there was no doubt of that, and in all the years Docie had known her, Clelia never suffered the lack of a thing she wanted. If her father's money paid all the liens and back taxes that amassed since Grandpa died, in those years when Docie and Thurman had struggled alone to save their farm from being swept away with the tide that carried everything else familiar and loved with it, Clelia had been big enough never to hold it over Thurman's head. With Docie herself it was another matter altogether: Docie was a buffer, absorbing the impact of Clelia's hints and carefully veiled implications concerning the source of their financial salvation. It had been a long labor, and Docie was worn thin with it now: the years had battered her past usefulness, and she could do no more. The love was all pressed out of her like the blood of grapes, only there was no wine to show for it.

Thurman would be all right, Docie reasoned. He had a fine old farm to show for his life's work and a crop of sturdy children and grandchildren. Old age had mellowed out for him into a rich field of ripening grain, and the harvest at the end of his days would be a good one. Docie felt it like a prophecy and bowed her head with the thought. Her disappearance would be a mere ripple in the otherwise tranquil prospect of Thurman's future.

Clelia would be glad she was gone, happy to be relieved of the burden of a dotty old maid with heart trouble into the bargain. Any irregularity in her sister-in-law, any peculiarity or faint resistance to her regime, Clelia chalked up to the arrhythmia that had plagued Docie since her youth. Docie always felt there was a double unkindness in her malady: it subjected her to Clelia's condescensions at every turn, and yet it had never been quite thorough enough to finish her off and settle the matter.

Docie closed her eyes and ground her teeth till her jaw ached. Perhaps Clelia was right: perhaps it *was* heart trouble. All of it.

She imagined the look on Clelia's face when she came in from her Missionary Union meeting and found the house empty and the strawberries spoiling in the heat on the kitchen table. Clelia had bought them right off the truck from Elizabeth Reid's half-witted son and remarked over her shoulder as she left for her meeting that someone had best make preserves before they weren't fit to eat. Which meant, of course, that she expected Docie do it without delay.

As Clelia's ponderous old Lincoln roared to life in the carport, something snapped inside of Docie. She couldn't quite say what did it. It might have been the look of calm triumph on Clelia's face as she turned at the door with some final instructions that Docie was too benumbed to comprehend, or the horrid blue bottle flies that were already drifting in at the open window and swarming dizzily above the strawberries, or the blood-red stain the berries had made through their flat on Clelia's favorite tablecloth. The cloth was hideously splotched with overblown hydrangeas in shades that nature never knew, and Docie hated it with a passion all out of proportion to its offense. The massive oak linen press in the hall was stuffed with beautiful things that had belonged to her mother and grandmother—lovely faded vintage prints and hand-worked cloths and turkey red damask—that suited the old-fashioned rooms with a self-effacing dignity, but Clelia forbade Docie to use them. Instead, Docie had borne with Clelia's tasteless hydrangeas and their equally tacky counterparts these fifty-odd years, and suddenly, like the startling recoil of a spring long-since stretched past its limit, she drew back from it all with an intensity that made her head spin. Something fundamental gave a great crack deep down inside of her, and she was done.

She wriggled out of her bib apron, dropping it on the ground where she stood, and without pausing to change out of her house shoes, she walked out the kitchen door and across the yard to the bull lot. The hens had all come running, waddling towards her with greedy clucks of pleasure, anticipating treats and kitchen scraps, but she waded through them without so much as a word. On her favorite, the pearl-white Araucana, she had bestowed a calm look and a sad ghost of a smile, but the hen had scattered with the others before her purposeful stride.

And now, here she was, at the limit of the property, before a forgotten gate, contemplating a view of green swale framed in feathery cedar and the needles of longleaf pine. She placed her hand on the gatepost and drank in the view: a low ribbon of richness wandering away eastward and flanked on all sides by dark oaks and silver-trunked elms. She felt the prickle of cedar against her cheek from a low-hanging bough and heard the low, heartbreaking murmur of a dove far down the hill. The valley had always been haunted by the mourning doves; rather ominously, she thought in later years, like the fateful and far-off melody of some unseen Piper beguiling youth away in his train. But the desolation could never efface the glory that had been. The place seemed to tingle and teem with the memory of it; Docie felt it must be a very thin veil indeed that fluttered between what had once been and what now was. The wind touched her face, bearing the blended perfume of honey-suckle and fresh-cut hay, and the veil wavered and parted slightly. Docie clenched the gatepost until her knuckles were white and caught her breath with a sob that fell upon the quiet like a low whimper of pain.

Jack Cowart had given her a ring here and told her of the adventures they were going to have together, out there in the great world. And when they had seen it all and done all that was to be done, they would come back here, and he would build a house for them on his father's land, in this very valley. The place was magic, he told her, and they would never grow old. And she believed him.

Docie leaned against the post and stared her past in the face with the composure long years had given her. Anger and rebellion had eventually burned themselves out, like a wildfire at the limit of a stream, and acceptance had brooded and built and grown in their place. It was the underpinning of all the future joists and timbers of her life, the foundation upon which she placed one weary brick of a day after another. And if a watercourse yet flowed in unseen caverns beneath that plain edifice, there was nothing on the surface to suggest of its existence.

But how different things would have been if Jack had lived! She remembered the wildness of her grief the night he died; she had wept it out here with her face in the grass, pounding her misery into the earth till her arms ached and she was exhausted and Grandma had come and steered her back to the house like a lost calf. She wondered now at the energy of that old passion; it seemed so foreign a thing to the years of weariness and stone-faced acceptance she'd known since. And yet, even as she wondered over it, some parched place seemed to widen within her—perhaps the very chasm that Clelia had so unwittingly opened with her silly presumption over the strawberries—and Docie heard the sound of far-off water, roiling and hissing on dry earth.

She looked down at the post and remembered Jack's hand upon it, young and determined. Then, stooping a little, she leaned forward and placed a kiss on its lichened surface.

The gate was grown over with honeysuckle vines, and she tore them away until she could pry an opening to accommodate her thin frame. She wedged herself in, and as she did, a childhood memory darted through her with a thrill so keen it felt like joy. Her grandmother read *Pilgrim's Progress* to them as children until the pages were falling out of the book—they knew it so well that she and Thurman used to act it out with their friends here in this very place. But as she scraped through the narrow opening and felt the rough wood against her papery skin, something shone out that had been incomprehensible to her before. She always loved the part of the story where Christian passed the Wicket Gate, leaving his old life behind. But she suddenly remembered how, at the last minute, Good Will reached out his hand and snatched him through with an astonishing deliverance. Docie took a deep draught of what felt like that very grace on the other side of the gate. For the first time in her life, she knew exactly how Christian felt.

Docie closed the latch carefully and set off through the tall grass down into the valley. Her stride seemed to lengthen and grow young even as she walked; she felt slender and supple-limbed and vital. She looked down at her faded and ugly house dress, and it was a short, light frock of cornflower blue. She felt the drab grey hair pinned against her head and touched a crop of waving gold. She kicked off her shoes and laughed a peal of silver bells, a flock of white doves startling up for joy. *Was this what it felt like to die?* To come back into one's self—to be *more* selved and more alive than the living could imagine? Was youth just a promise of eternity, a brief candle-flare of things to come? She felt her very fingertips thrill with the truth of it, and when she glanced at her hands, she half-expected to see gleams of light shooting out of them and darting off the shimmering grass before her. The very young and the very old—they were both so close upon the fringes of eternity. She remembered that now and felt it in herself as a present truth. The unseen things were so near, perhaps more real than anything else.

The vision faded but the strange lightness remained. She dug her hands down into the pockets of her worn dress. She felt the grass unsheathing its cool blades between her toes. It occurred to her that she hadn't walked barefoot like this since she was a girl, and she laughed again at the thought. There were daisies here, modest maidens of early summer, and she remembered that she and Jack's sister, Cassie, had made crowns of them by the armload. With a slight lifting of her chin and a blue spark kindling in her eyes, she smiled at the memory and fingered one of the flowers in passing. Only the young picked flowers; the old knew their span was brief enough.

The walk down into the valley was a cleansing thing; Docie felt its healing touch like the dew of the morning. There was a baptismal freshness in the breeze and the remembrances it evoked, a retroactive mercy rushing back over past sorrows and drowning them with joy—joy that she had *lived*. She had been alive to know love and pain and all the graces that lay between. The years vanished, and her heart quickened to the unique song that had been sung over her life since her infancy. It wasn't near enough to distinguish as actual notes and sounds, but she recognized it, even from afar. She had been haunted by it all her life, even when she most doubted having heard it at all.

Docie sniffed with satisfaction: the air was grass-sweet and slightly bovine. Jack's father only occasionally ran his herd here, and when he had, her youthful imagination had transformed them into the encroaching hordes of an enemy host which she and the Cowart children had hidden from in the tall grass. She smiled with the memory, but as she stepped deeper into the valley and it opened before her, she caught sight of a dozen red forms hunched and reposing in the green shades below. Her smile widened, and then faded. The nearest red mass shifted its thunderous weight and lifted its head from the grass, revealing a graceful sweep of curving horns, bone-colored and tipped with black. Docie froze. Black Stuff was an exception; her whole life had groomed her for a healthy fear of bulls, particularly in company with cows. She glanced back the way she had come: it was straight up and far enough for the bull to overtake her if he chose. Her eyes darted to the left, down towards the hollow where the branch ran through. In her girlhood there had been a low fence to keep the cows out of a strip of woodland that Jack's father particularly loved. It was always falling over or in need of repair; it was one of the reasons this valley had usually been abandoned to the children and the daisies. There was no telling what shape it was in now, or if it even remained, but Docie had no choice. She clenched her hands at her sides and took a step forward.

The bull dipped its head and lifted it again with an action that made the blood freeze in her veins. Docie felt a surge of terror spring through her, cold as quicksilver, but she kept her wits. She took another cautious step or two and then held her breath as the bull returned its attention to the grass. Inch by inch she claimed her slow progress towards the hollow and the fence she prayed was still there. When she was directly opposite the bull, and nearly as close to it as she was to her longed-for haven, the creature suddenly looked up with a snort of indignation. The enormous head bobbed and swung from side to side and one of the fearsome hooves began to paw the ground in a gathering wrath. With her heart pounding in her ears, Docie started to run.

Gone was her late litheness as she panted and stumbled through the tall grass. She seemed to feel every moment of her seventy-nine years; they were grasping and tearing at her with merciless hands, dragging her back towards those terrible horns and thundering hooves. She could sense the tremor of the earth as the mighty thing overtook her, and she imagined its fire-hot breath drawing nearer by the moment. There was a boy in the county, a child she had known in school, who was gored by a bull—a hideous business which the parents and grandparents of her generation held up as a terrible ensign of the dangers of unmarked pastures. She thought of him now with a sickening clarity, enfleshing his very fear into her own as she ran for her life.

Life? Not an hour ago it had been inconsequential. Now it was a wild thing, desperate and defiant. The change was a mystery to her, dark and inscrutable like the holy things of God. She only knew that the death she envisioned at the wicket gate and coming down into the valley was freedom and light, a loss only of the burden of years and a gathering of fragments into a beautiful whole. But this was a swallowing up, a snuffing out, and it seemed that the whole universe reeled with the insistence that it must not be. A roar of pain went through her chest and shot down her left arm so that for one blinding moment she actually thought that the bull had gotten her. But with the pain came the great rushing of an unloosed flood. It boiled up from unimaginable depths and swirled over the dry riverbed of her heart. It seemed to lift and carry her, bearing her with a new strength. She ran as though a strong, young hand were helping her along, drawing and urging her faltering steps toward the fence, which she saw to her dizzying relief was still intact, though the posts leaned at crazy angles. She lurched forward hungrily as she drew near, then dropped to her knees at its limit, one hand grasping a fence post and the other outstretched to cushion her fall. Then, with an agonized glance over her shoulder, she ducked between the sagging lengths of barbed wire and rolled wearily out on the other side. The hem of her housecoat snagged on one of the barbs, but she was too fatigued to lift it off. The strong young hand was gone now, and she was an exhausted and dangerously spent old woman. But alive. The bull halted at the fence with an ominous grunt.

Docie lay there for some moments, unable to move, while the bull tossed its head and dug at the earth a few times for good measure. At length he gave up his quarry and ambled back to his herd, but still Docie lay, staring up into the patches of blue between the tree limbs. Her breath came in painful gulps, and her heart was pounding with irregular leaps and lulls. Her only discernible movement was the rising and falling of her calico-clad bosom and the occasional twitching of the fingers of her right hand as it lay outspread on the ground beside her.

"Lord-a-mercy," she whispered as her eyes fluttered shut.

It was as genuine a prayer as she ever uttered in her life, and even as she said it, she sensed it had already been answered. The great fear had torn through her like a summer storm, scattering chaff and debris before its wild onrush, and the unleashed waters had done the rest. It was the current of her heart's love, long buried and built over, but as she lay there, prone and helpless beneath the trees, she saw behind her closed eyes the careful bricks and beams of a safe existence crumbling in the flood. It carried off whole walls and floors of pretense, toppling her imitations of aliveness, and she gasped over the agony and the joy of it. And it was then that she realized it was not her own love that drove the stream at all, but Love itself. One great drop of it squeezed out the corner of her eye and ran down her wrinkled cheek.

She thought calmly of Thurman and the children, how fine they all were, and how many of them there were to love. She remembered her grandparents and smiled as another tear rolled down her face and dropped onto the leaves beside her head. She clutched after a dim memory of her mother and father, both dead before she was old enough to grieve, and her heart gave a great bound for them. She saw Jack's face as she had not seen it in decades, *centuries*, grinning at her in the old, boyish way. And as her mind turned gently to Clelia, she seemed to see her for the first time, bathed in the same clear tide that had rushed from her heart and spilled over all the others. Clelia as a child; Clelia as a young woman: hurting and fearful and afraid of her own disappointment. Docie's features softened with a new tenderness and she opened her eyes.

Of course. Why had she not seen it before? Her own pain must have blinded her to the gnawing anguish Clelia had known all these years. Clelia had lain down with it every night and gotten up with it every morning, and in her quiet frenzy, she turned her fury upon her sister-in-law, the only one she really wanted to hurt. Anger and fear—what relentless taskmasters they were! Docie always thought that Clelia had gotten everything she ever wanted out of life, that the powers that be had denied her nothing; she had a good husband and a beautiful old place and affectionate, successful children. And yet—Docie saw it now with the awful clarity which only great fear or great love can afford—there was one thing that Clelia had wanted, one thing withheld which had poisoned all the rest for her. And Docie Thaxter was the only woman on earth who would ever have it. Docie might have brought her hopes and her heart's love to Jack Cowart's grave, but Clelia had taken something away, something terrible and smoldering and cruel. And her life had been seething with it ever since.

Docie moaned and sat up. Poor Clelia! She needed more love than them all! She was famished for it—starving to death in the midst of a feast. And poor Thurman! He must never know it. A great throb of compassion seized Docie and warmth spread through her limbs and over her body, as if the shock had settled the mad mutiny of her heartbeat and brought it back into rhythm. She struggled to her feet with one thought in her mind. There was an old creek bed, a dried channel of the branch, that snaked through the hollow and up the hill to the fence line of Thurman's north pasture. The climb was arduous after the day's adventures, and she felt like a pilgrim in very deed as the stones and dried twigs of the runnel tore at her bare feet. But at length she reached the top, and squirming herself through another span of barbed wire, she set off down the slope to the house.

Black Stuff was there, grazing placidly as any of his dames, and Docie gave him a deferential nod as she passed. It was all she had time for: there was much work to do. She crossed the yard and went straight into the kitchen, letting the old screened door slam behind her with a wail and a bang. She picked up her apron from the floor and went over to the table to inspect the stain on Clelia's cloth. She waved the flies off the strawberries then lifted the flat and whisked the cloth out from under it.

When it was airing in the yard, under a paste of salt and lemon juice, she came back into the kitchen and went at the strawberries as if they were the great labor of her life. Indeed, for that very moment they were: the ruby-colored juice that ran down her fingers might just as well have been her heart's blood. After they were in the pot, simmering their incense up into the sweltering kitchen, she watched with the careful devotion of a prayer. It was that important—it was *all* that important.

An hour later when Clelia came in from her meeting, Docie was just lifting the last gleaming jar out of the hot water bath and setting it on a spotless white kitchen towel with the others. She turned with a smile for her sister-in-law and looked her straight in the eye.

"Hello, Clelia," she said.

Clelia took in the scene, her eyes traveling over the room as if in search of something to disapprove of. When she encountered Docie's gaze, her own eyes narrowed slightly and then faltered. She looked at the ground for a moment, as if to recover herself from the fearsome and unflinching thing she had seen in her sister-in-law's face. It was both adamant and appealing, and she had a sudden wild fear that it would never let her go.

Then her eyes shot back up again with a faint gleam.

"Theodocia Thaxter! Why on God's earth are you barefoot?"

"I see the mole. I see his tiny hill. I think about his blind eyes and his dark world of emptiness and earth. I am the mole. I light a cigarette and stare at the nothingness before me."

—ALBERT CAMUS, Stranger to Meaningful Existence (WNI)

PAYING ATTENTION
by Andrew Peterson

Pay attention to the little things.
Pay attention to the big things too,
Because both are easy enough to miss,
And are one and the same more often than not.

Pay attention to the eerie silence
When the air conditioner cycles off
And the only sound is the creak of the house.
Pay attention to the clank and rumble

Of the freight train as it wobbles by.
Pay attention to birds—the ones that tweet,
The ones that honk, and the ones
That lie dead in the road. Notice them.

Notice the level of the creek before the rain
And after. Remember that the water

Rushing around your ankles was a cloud
Not so long ago, a cloud that began

Somewhere in Alaska, perhaps, and before that,
A dark, frigid, and silent subterranean sea.
Then notice the minnows pecking at your toes.
Pay attention to the turns your life has taken

To bring you to the place you now stand.
Most blessings sprout not from the plans
We make, but from the soil of their sad ruin.
Watch their slow, unstoppable unraveling,

Their disassembly, the final shudder, and
Their collapse, and the dustcloud that follows.
Pay attention then to the way your heart
Breathes a sigh of relief when the work

That was never yours anyway is lifted
From your tired hands. Pay attention,
When you clean up the mess, to the treasure
That the wreck unearthed, and give thanks

For your folly and God's favor.

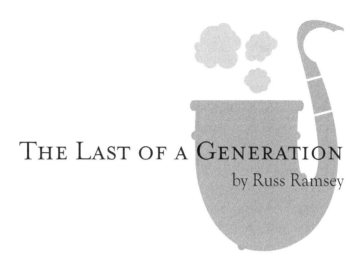

THE LAST OF A GENERATION
by Russ Ramsey

ARRIVAL

The tires under the right wing touched the ground for a split second before a gust of wind thrust us back into the air. The turbulence tilted our plane like a toy in a child's hand.

Manhattan lay to my left, Newark to my right.

As quickly as it had come, the wind dissipated, dropping us back down to the tarmac. The pilot opened the flaps to pin us down and brought us to a stop in a land I had only visited once as boy—New York, New York.

Prior to landing, the captain informed us that Newark had put us in a holding pattern over the city because of a strong westerly gale. The wind forced all of the air traffic to funnel onto one secondary north-to-south runway. To attempt another route would have been too dicey, so we circled high above, peering out the windows at the cramped streets and high-rises of the Five Boroughs below.

So this was New York? This was where my mother grew up. Did this mean that somewhere, buried in the prologue to my life, was the detail that I hailed from the unfamiliar steel, brick, and mortar of this city? If you had asked me, I would have told you I'm from the cornfields of Indiana. That was where I grew up, and my father, and his father before him. Almost all my childhood memories were set there: the first time I fell in love and, as the story inevitably goes, the first time I learned my heart could break; the time I saw *The Karate Kid* and left the theater believing I had just been trained in the martial arts; the first and only time I ever punched a kid in the face, and the first and only time a kid punched me. Neither of us deserved it.

I also remember the glint of my Nana and Pop Pop's silver Subaru station wagon as they turned up our gravel road. I remember how it would disappear in the cloud of dust it kicked up. I remember pressing my nose against our living room window, watching and waiting for that car to once again come into view so my brother and I could race outside to meet them in the driveway. We did this because when they came to visit they always brought us presents. We figured if we could carry their bags, one of us might spot them. And as any kid can tell you, locating a gift is half the battle.

Last summer, Nana died. She lived to be eighty-nine. In her final months she went from being a strong, proper, educated, former French teacher to being a digni-fied yet frail woman with a childlike manner who had regained an appreciation for simpler things, like taking rides in the car or playing Go Fish.

Nana was born at the beginning of the roaring '20s—a decade punctuated by the Stock Market Crash of 1929. She was nine years old when the bottom fell out. She was born before the advent of the telephone, the refrigerator, and the traffic light; before the band-aid, FM radio, and the Model T Ford; before penicillin, nylon, television, and the zipper. She was eleven when the Empire State Building was completed and the Star-Spangled Banner was named our national anthem. She was twenty-one when the Japanese bombed Pearl Harbor. She lived through World War II, saw the civil rights movement, the Korean War, and Vietnam. Her life spanned fifteen different presidential administrations.

Pop Pop died several years earlier. Uncle Gordon before that. Great Grandma Brown before that. And now Nana. She was the last of her generation, and I had come to New York to lay her to rest.

As if we were standing in a line formed this side of eternity's gate, when Nana stepped on through, the rest of us took another step forward. Now my kids are the ones with their noses pressed against the window, watching for my parents to arrive so they can meet them in the driveway and begin their less than subtle search for presents.

For the first time in my life I feel like I can reach out and almost touch eternity's door.

I hadn't come to New York just to oversee the passing of a generation, though. I had also come with my mother to explore their city. She had it all mapped out. We would set out on foot to walk the streets of New York, immersed in the sights and sounds and smells of the city that was as much a character in our story as it was a place on a map. We would ride the Staten Island Ferry where Pop Pop courted Nana every day on their commute to work in Manhattan, we'd run our fingers over the numbers on the house on Fingerboard Road where they lived when my mother was born, we'd stand in the lobby of the Hippodrome Building where my mom and dad first noticed each other while working for Eastern Airlines. She was giving me the day as a gift filled with images I had never seen, images that were slowly fading a little more each day.

Once the plane came to a stop, the stewardess suggested that we might want to thank the pilot for his skillful landing. We all clapped. We all meant it, too. The bell sounded and the cabin lights came on. I slung my backpack over my shoulder, cleared the jet way, and stepped out into the city that never sleeps.

GROUND TRANSPORTATION

You're the boss, Boss," Desmond the Concierge said when I asked if I could leave my bags with him at the hotel and pick them up later. Mom and I were headed into the city for the day and wouldn't be back before checkout. When he handed me my claim ticket, he also gave me a map of New York City's ground transportation. For that I gave him two dollars.

We mapped our passage to midtown Manhattan: we'd take the hotel shuttle to the airport's air train, the air train to the city train, the city train to Penn Station, and we'd set off on foot from there. This was our plan.

Coming up from the underground of Penn Station, we stepped into a labyrinth of towering stone, glass, and steel. The city offered us long corridors of vision down the avenues and cross streets around us. Though we could see so much from where we were standing, we knew it was just a sliver of all that was there. I began to suspect that while this city had much to show me, infinitely more would stay hidden.

The terrain before me was at the same time abundant and deficient, absurd and elegant—teeming with its history of bondage and liberty, tragedy and triumph. No one with a simple story had ever walked these streets. But then no one has a simple story, do they?

The homeless, the newlyweds, the cashiers at Macy's, and the tourists are all pressed in, shoulder to shoulder, beholding the same metropolitan maze, though their interpretations are worlds apart. There are the poor with their sad tales of their paths to poverty, and there are the rich with even sadder stories of their ascents to wealth. The prodigals of the Midwest are there, living it up in the distant country—some dining at Central Park's Tavern on the Green, flush with cash, tipping the cabbies and waiters without a second thought, while others scrounge the dumpsters out back, scripting their apologies and begging for just enough cash to get back home.

And then there's me. I'm the boss, Boss.

Mom tells me we need to get some perspective. So off we go to the observation deck of the Empire State Building, eighty-six stories up. The crowds are negligible so we're able to choose our views of the city at will. Manhattan looks stacked and compressed, as if its shoreline is held in place by a belt cinched tight. If it ever breaks, look out!

Mom shows me where we're headed—first north, up Broadway to Central Park, then south by way of 5th Avenue. From Rockefeller Plaza, we'll catch the subway to Ground Zero, and then hop aboard the Staten Island Ferry for a quick there-and-back-again, just as Nana and Pop Pop had done so many years before.

So off we go. We see Times Square, the Ed Sullivan Theater, and the Rainbow Room. We enter Central Park from the west and leave from the east. I lunch on the most wonderful and obscene pastrami on rye I've ever laid eyes on. Then we head over to St. Patrick's Cathedral. An inclination to repent of that pastrami on rye comes over me as we sit for a moment in the solemn beauty of the old oak and stained glass.

We all know New York City is big. And historic. And expensive. We can get all that from a fly-over, or the internet, or the travel channel. But I'm on the ground. I'm in the thick of it. My senses are popping with sights and smells and sounds and textures all coming at me all at once.

What do I see, Boss?

This city is a parable—a paradox of stain and polish. Every surface is at the same time worn smooth and covered in grime; both, I presume, from the same thing—us. I walk a sidewalk where the feet of a billion pilgrims have gone before me. I hold a railing smudged by ten billion distinct fingerprints. At the bow of the ferry, I sit on a bench that has taken the weight of countless others just like me and as different from me as you can imagine. And together we have worn away every surface, have polished them smooth. We've picked up the messiness of one another's existence wherever we've gone and from whatever we've touched. And we've left behind bits of the crud we brought in with us—from the lifeless dust that falls off our feet to the living oils that flow from the pores of our fingers and foreheads.

The Steelworkers Union may have constructed the city's frame, but the huddled masses painted it. Every footfall, every scuff of every steamer trunk pulled across every granite floor, every try of a door handle, every tire, horseshoe, subway wheel, rickshaw, and hot dog cart has left its mark. You'll never see it, but I'm certain I left mine. We can't go anywhere without leaving either a mark or a mess. And yet, neither can we single-handedly ruin the place. We step out onto the riskiest edges of what we imagine our lives can bear only to find them worn smooth by a million other fools who have also cantilevered themselves out there and found they somehow hold.

The subway takes us to Battery Park. We join the throngs waiting to board the ferry for Staten Island. To the west I see Ellis Island—that port of inspection and admittance into the New World. Appearing equal parts sanctuary, cemetery, prison, hospital, and monastery, and devoid of any hint of whimsy, an aura of seriousness hangs over the island—as it should. From 1892 to 1954, all the immigrants who set foot on that ground carried with them reasons weighty enough to leave behind their known old world for this unknown new one. From the steamship they'd follow the walkway to the inspection center and climb the Stairs of Separation, where immigration officials would scan the crowds looking for signs of illness. Under the scrutiny of these officers, immigrants silently ascended the separation stairs knowing clammy skin, runny noses, or bloodshot eyes could have been more than enough cause to pluck any one of them from the tired and poor yearning to breathe free and send them back where they came from.

From London to Kalmar, from Wittenberg to Geneva, from Paris to Cologne, and for reasons all their own, men and women, young and old, bet it all on a perilous passage across the open sea to this little island of assessment, knowing it was all for nothing if they couldn't make it through to the mainland.

Serious business, indeed.

Tomorrow we'll head over to Metuchen, New Jersey, to pay our respects to Nana—a woman of both stain and polish. You don't make it to eighty-nine without making your share of messes. But she certainly polished away some of my rough edges, too.

Tomorrow my parents will officially graduate to the generational position that Nana was the last of hers to hold, and I will step into the one my mom and dad have held since the day I was born. We're not beginning again. We're just shuffling up a step in the line. And we're treading sacred ground whether we know it or not.

But that's tomorrow. First things first. The PATH Train will take us from Ground Zero to the airport, and the hotel shuttle will take me back to Desmond, who will give me back my luggage.

And for that I will give him another two dollars.

187

Departure

The cornerstone by the entrance to the church in Metuchen, New Jersey, reads: "1717."

Think about that.

What am I, I wonder as I cross the threshold, *the millionth person to enter this building?*

I imagine the stoic, patronizing, agnostic husband coming to church because his wife got religion. He hopes this too shall pass.

And there's the young man who is only there because the last time he visited this church he saw *her*, the girl of his dreams. But just like that, she slipped away after the service. So he returns Sunday after Sunday hoping to see her again.

There's the young mother, who just lost her husband in the Civil War. She's locking arms with her husband's grieving, also-widowed mother. What will they do now?

There's the swaddled baby, the toddler missing her nap, the fresh-faced boy with two pockets filled with living bits of mischief he took from the earth when no one was watching. He's got plans.

There's the grandmother who, to her recollection, hasn't missed more than a few Sundays in five decades of worship. She prays for every new face she sees—earnest prayers.

There's the nervous bride in the sitting room and her groom back in the vestry. They're on the verge of promising their lives to each other and making it all legal.

There are the potlucks in the yard, the voting booths lining the narthex, and the civic groups planning their holiday fundraisers in the children's Sunday school room as they sit on chairs a size too small for their bad backs and large butts.

There are the alcoholics taking their steps to recovery, praying for the ability to know the difference between what they can control and what they cannot.

There's the teenage girl wondering if she should keep the baby, the boyfriend to her right without a clue, the father to her left about to find out, and the mother next to him who already knows because, well, she just knows. She dabs a tear from her eye but no one notices.

I imagine that if this place was built nearly three hundred years ago, then it has seen most any situation that has ever led anyone anywhere to darken the door of a church.

Me? Death brought me.

Nana's memorial service is familiar in its unfamiliarity—a collection of strangers bound to one another by blood but separated by time and space, mostly only seeing each other when someone gets married or someone dies. These days, it's usually when someone dies.

We reintroduce ourselves. We all look at bit older since last we met. We try to remember where we left our conversations. Then we remember we left them at the last funeral. We say we really need to meet on happier occasions, but if we're honest we know we'll probably never make those arrangements.

I open the memorial service by inviting the dozen or so gathered to think about any remembrances they might wish to share about Nana. We sing a couple of old hymns. I deliver a short eulogy, and we open the floor for a few stories and poems.

From there, we adjourn to the fellowship hall. Over the years, as this church's property has yielded to progress, the original sanctuary has expanded to add a wing of classrooms, offices, and the small chapel where we gathered to remember Nana. Filling the yard to the east of the sanctuary is a cemetery with ghost-white limestone markers dating back before the Civil War. They stand tall, thin, and rounded. I see one that actually bears the inscription "R.I.P."

When it came time to build a fellowship hall, the land to the west was already developed to capacity. So they built a stand-alone structure on the east side of the cemetery. The strange effect is that for a person to go from the fellowship hall to worship, they have to pass through the center of this garden of graves.

As we walk, my cousin points at a headstone bearing my mother's maiden name—Aspinwall. I don't recognize the first name, but whoever he is, I know if I could go back far enough I'd find a part of his story that is also a part of mine. Traces of the genes that cut my jaw, colored my eyes, and parted my hair lie buried in the earth beneath my feet.

Just like the others, this headstone offers nothing but a name and a date. Yet for every pilgrim moving between the fellowship of men and the sanctuary of God, these headstones—like a choir half buried, half rising from the dead—sing the same refrain: For everything there is a season, and a time for every matter under heaven: a time to be born, a time to die, and a time for the life that happens in between.

After the reception, we head off to Staten Island to see the large brownstone building where Nana went to high school. I try to picture Nana as a teenager, but I can't. From there we drive over to the house my mom lived in as a baby. I try to imagine her as a child and realize I've never done this before. I've never imagined her as anyone other than my mother. Have I really never seen her as anything but a part of the supporting cast in my story? What about *her* first love? Her first broken heart? Her first fight? I hadn't even wondered about these things until I stood on the sidewalk in front of the house at 72 Fingerboard Road. There are parts of my own mother's story as unknown to me as the story of the Aspinwall buried in that Metuchen grave. And I realize there will be parts of mine that she'll never know either.

Though there are and will always be gaps in what we know of each other's stories, there are sacred stretches where our paths converge and we walk a few seasons together. And that's what mom and I are doing here in New York. We're talking about death, life, faith, and regret as we pound the pavement like a couple of detectives piecing together a timeline and digging up clues that shed light on the truth of who we are and where we're from.

Mom observes there are only a few of us left who would ever take this particular tour. It's our story—no one else's. We wonder how many of the people we've passed in the last seventy-two hours were doing the same thing. We wonder if, in some small way, the answer is everyone.

As the day grows late, I've had enough. I have a plane to catch, and I don't want to miss my departure. Though the GPS insists the Newark Airport is less than ten miles away, I have spent the past three days learning, if nothing else, that things around here take time. It's time to go.

HOME

At last, I am home.

I have a three-year-old named Jane. She's got her little hands on my cheeks. She's looking into my eyes. She wants my attention. It's time for her nap. And being Sunday afternoon, it's time for mine too. She tells me she is going to get her purple blanket and crawl into my bed to wait for me. She wants to snuggle. With that she skips away.

I don't have all the time in the world. One day I will leave this fellowship of the saints I love so much, and I will step across that threshold into an eternal sanctuary of exultant praise in the presence of the Maker and Lover of my soul. Between the two I will be buried. People will gather and offer words in my memory. They will lay my body down in a grave and my headstone will rise from the dirt and join the chorus in the land of the living, singing: "A time to be born, a time to die, a time to live again."

Perhaps I will outlive the others and die as the last of my generation. And if my little Jane lives long enough, maybe she will be the last of hers, outliving her brother and sisters. Maybe she will prompt some young father I'll never meet to reflect upon his grandmother's passing. Since there is a time for every matter under heaven, there may be a time for this.

But for right now, the matter under heaven calling for my attention is a little girl with a purple blanket, burrowing down under the covers in the land of the living. She is happy and warm. And she is waiting for me.

One day I will take the boat to Ellis Island. I'll walk the pier and enter the station. I'll see the stacks of abandoned steamer trunks, the rejection papers under glass, the black and white photos of the mustachioed men in their bowler hats and the women with their parasols. I'll study their eyes, looking for hints of their hope,

191

their fear, their desperation. I'll try to imagine them standing on that same floor, not browsing a museum, but looking for a new world.

I'll climb the Separation Stairs and I'll think of Jesus' parable of the sheep and the goats. I'll think about what it means to be a citizen of a Kingdom I must leave everything to enter. I'll understand that I, too, am an immigrant.

ON THE IRON BAR AND THE PRICE YOU PAY, JAMES DEAN

by Don Chaffer

For a season we lived as wild animals,
As boxes of unmarked mail,
As kites fluttered loose from strings,
As bottlerockets, whistling into fantastic finales.
And we sailed over cities at pinpoint height,
Skipping along sky-ways,
Far from the friends of our tethered days,
Those sidewalkers and cardrivers.

We spoke as howler monkeys
With force and volume—senseless as sex, crude as oil—
In long, resounding whoops,
And fine, barbaric yawps.

And it seemed to be going okay.

We were cigarettes on work breaks.
We were vodka cranberry.
We were shuddering fingers on guitar strings,
And stuttering sticks on drum skins.

Whip-its in the walk-in freezer,
Ritalin-flavored truck stop chicken fried steaks,
And greasy songs in the parking lot, arm in arm,
Just waiting for someone to call us hippie fags,
So we could bare our teeth.

It all seemed so good that it wasn't worth wondering
How long it might last.
It would just last, man.
We were good, thank you,
And yes, another round,
And yes, the Rolling Stones,
And yes, I know how to dance,
And no, not right now,
And man, do you remember that?
And no, I don't,
And I know, isn't that crazy?

And we would just keep laughing.
It was so great to laugh.
It was probably the best part.
When we were laughing, it seemed like:

> The field sobriety test would never come,
> Like the lights would just stay on by themselves,
> And the stove would just turn off, you know,
> Automatically,
> And we could just keep fighting,
> And no one would ever really get hurt.

And I loved the idea of it.
I was a founding father, high on democracy.
I was Jimmy calling from the crack house.

I was don't-you-feel-it-don't-you-feel-it-don't-you-feel-it (?)
I was in all the way.

And now:

>   My name comes up for jury duty.
>   I get word that we need more diapers and milk.
>   The applause fades,
>   The curfew bell rings,
>   And when I want to stay out late to sing Woody Guthrie,
>   I don't.

And of course New York is still New York,
And Las Vegas is still Las Vegas.
But no one here cares anymore.
Somebody else will have to do those things for a while.

The young howlers
Will knock the older ones out of the top of the tree.
They will call for the females,
They will swing with impossible grace,
And you will just write a poem,
And you will just read it late at night
By the glow of the bedside lamp,
And afterward, go to check on the sleeping children.

(Those funny open mouths,
Tumble-tossed limbs,
And tender breaths,
Stretched, loose and lazy,
Across coteries of bears and dogs,
Leftover Legos, and Barbie clothes.
All suspended in the air

with such impossible innocence.
There may be nothing more beautiful than a sleeping child.)

Then, you will sit by the fish tank
And wonder how you came to be so pushed out
And pushed in all at once,
How you could be so coming of age,
And so long in the tooth.

Don't worry, James Dean.
We will usher you out of cool
And into old age.
You will become the father you once longed to hold,
And when it collapses on you—the weight of goodness—
You will love the crush of it.
It will not be so bad becoming someone after all.
You will begin to feel the iron rod inside,
Running straight along your supple spine, and you will think,
Okay, now I am standing up straight,
And you will be.
I swear it.

Even nervous and uncomfortable
    (These people seem so normal),
Even daydreaming of detective shows on the computer in bed
    (This day is so long),
Even when you keep your mouth shut
For the sake of newfound civility
    (I cannot believe this).

Even then you will be standing up straight, James Dean.

You want to know how I know?

You want to know the secret of it all?
Well, here it is:

It never looks as straight as it feels,
And it never feels as straight as it looks.

You never get to see yourself
You just keep looking over your shoulder in the mirror,
And not really seeing the back of your own head.
Sure.
You could get another mirror,
And look in that mirror at the other mirror
And then you'd see the back of you clearly
But then you'd also see yourself behind yourself,
And behind him, another you,
And another, and another
Until it makes you nauseous.

So, you put down your beer,
And you say, "Boys, I'm gonna pack it in.
I got an early tee time tomorrow."

You get in your car.
You turn on the radio.
They will be playing
"Take the Money and Run" by The Steve Miller Band.
You will think,

Now, that was a great summer band.

And you will listen to that rhythm section
Stumble through whole passages like
A teenage boy on a basketball court,

And think,

      Yeah.
      A great summer band.

And then, you will shut off the radio
Before the last chorus plays,
To listen to the sound of the road's
Deep-throated hum
As your car hurtles through the winter night.

Then, James Dean,
You are sitting up straight as an arrow.

But thank God you don't notice
Because the moon is out,
And it's pouring silvery light on the fields by the highway again,

And I would hate for you to miss that.

WALKING ON WATER
by Eric Peters

I have walked on water.

In truth, I ran. I was an adolescent, maybe fourteen at the time, and my childhood buddy, Stanford, had a three-wheeled ATV that we often rode in the lot behind his house. The lot was a large communal ground shared by surrounding neighbors, and in one particular spot, a cluster of sweet gums, tallow, small oaks, and underbrush had intertwined their roots to form a fortified grove. It was there that, over the course of seemingly endless summer afternoons, we cut out a trail of ruts and turns, constructed forts, and converted the area into a young boy's panacea. When it rained, the rutted trails became a quagmire, a temporary bayou, a place scarcely resembling its dry-weather self, and it was in that flooded Eden that I once walked on peanut butter-colored swamp water.

One of those summer afternoons, after a typical Louisiana downpour, Stanford and I were riding the ATV, churning our way through the knee-high water of the grove. It was all mirth and high adventure until an unexpected bump—a root perhaps—thrust our front wheel upward, sending us into wheelie formation. I was seated behind Stanford, and in an effort to avoid falling backward I instinctively jumped off, landing feet first in the knee-deep, murky water. In my fear of actual and imagined snakes, I panicked. I was in such a hurry to escape that I hold little doubt I ran atop the liquid surface. Stanford cried with hysterical laughter at the spectacle: me high-stepping across the water in utter, inexplicable, and self-inflicted terror. It may or may not have been a miracle, but it is certainly a farcical memory.

My attempts to escape from reality did not end that day in a storm-swollen neighborhood swamp. My story of escape is perpetual, a tale replete with caustic and Pyrrhic results. Five years ago, I began my one-way transition into fatherhood, and though it has not been without joy, finding a healthy balance between life as a father and life as a performing, traveling musician is a persistent struggle. I hit the road and play concerts for a living, returning home each time to resume life in the presence of two spirited young boys. The reentry is never easy. In a sense, I am constantly leaving one chaos for another. As I traverse these wildly different realms, I wax and wane between periods of guilt and shame, rarely able to partake of the joy apparent on the surface. When I am on the road, the guilt I feel for my beloved wife, left alone to tend to our children, is massive. Alternately, when I am home, the guilt and shame I feel that I am not out earning a consistent, weekly wage is equally burdensome. I am a back-and-forth disaster. Rare is my contentment. My overriding psychological state is one of stress, of feeling out of control, of being locked inside a cage. The waters rise. I watch my feet disappear beneath the floodwater, and I panic. Wanderlust tugs at my sleeve as I grapple with domestic life, seeking to balance an unconventional career with a normal family. I become increasingly irritable, desiring to be left alone, striving to prevent myself from falling backward, and I sink beneath the waves, my mind no longer able to imagine miracles, much less a bright world.

In my attempts to escape from quotidian life, from monotony, from the dull blanket of acedia, I become overwhelmed, succumbing to apathy. I sink beneath the surface and disappear into the silent oblivion of self-absorption, self-pity, and, ironically, imaginary bliss. As if plunged into a pit, I watch helplessly as darkness explodes upward, enveloping, thickening, and encircling. Filaments of light dot the heights as distant, pale, unreachable boundaries. The darkness loiters as a familiar and unwelcome guest; it clings to me, pinned on like Eeyore's tail. It is an inexplicable melancholy, an ever-present sadness, an unscalable wall, a friend that is no friend, a companion that offers no company, a love whose only gift is loathing.

I came face to face with an unavoidable Jericho wall one summer not long past. Together with my family, I was working at a youth camp in the mountains of north Georgia. I was surrounded by a group of thoughtful, giving, humorous people. It was an oasis where happiness, rest, and clarity should have thrived in my heart—yet I was the antithesis of all these. Anxiety gripped me, took its toll, imposed upon me an unbearable pressure that urged me to lean into the lying voices in my head and heart. Though ably cared for within a closely knit and welcoming community, I felt as alone as I ever had, unable to summon the clarity or hope to see myself as anything other than a complete and utter failure, a monumental waste of anyone's time, King Midas in reverse. The wall loomed before me, just as immense and impenetrable as that which confronted the Israelites encamped at Jericho, and succumbing to deflated hope and failing self-confidence, I believed that the world would be better off without me, that everything I touched was destined to turn into a mess, that I was wholly unnecessary. Anxiety-plagued and drowning in an illogical cycle of despair, I was barely able to perform my only job, that of musician. Asked to make a simple cameo appearance on stage, to join in the levity of a programmatic moment, I could not even muster the courage to stand in front of an audience. At the moment I was asked, I recall being utterly overwhelmed by such a request. I was unable to answer, shaking my head in confusion, and I walked away from the scene. In many ways I forgot how to smile or to take interest in anyone. I retreated from social settings, preferring to disappear into isolation. I found that holding a book was much easier than holding a conversation. I cast no shadow because I, myself, was the shadow. I was sinking in the swamp once again, engulfed in the emotional flood of my own depression. I imagined the snakes—the judgments and disapproval of others—and felt them slithering in around me. But I could not understand, much less explain, my baffling paralysis.

To say that light had departed from my world—or that I had departed from the light—is only a micron of the whole. I found myself confronted with a thought that I hoped I would never have to utter, much less act on. I was certain that, with the exception of my wife and two boys, the world would be better off without me, that my presence on earth was inconsequential, that I did not matter, either in spirit or in flesh. Surely our human nature presupposes disheartening seasons, times when nothing goes right, when dreams crash and we burn out. However, to believe that one's own spirit is inconsequential, that it is irrelevant, that it has no good gift to give—that is a leap far beyond the mere supposal of a rainy day. One evening that summer, exhausted, empty, fearful, and curled in bed, I admitted those thoughts to my wife. And I knew as the words left my lips that not only was I in need of help, but I needed to seek that help out, to race high-stepping across the swamp for safety, for health, for light, for—my God!—any hope of rescue.

Depression. The image is of a hole in the earth, a patch of ground sunken below the horizon. It is a valley of glue, hindering any forward motion. Once a traveler has fallen within it, no matter the surrounding beauty, the eyes are blindfolded. The traveler is made prisoner to apathy, able only to focus inward—on darkness, on loss, on disappointment, on perceived failure, on shame at being passed over, on the all-consuming despair within. The secret sadness of depression swallows light, quenches hope, scuttles it amid endless waves of shadow.

Disappointment. When we are young we believe we are born—destined!—to conquer the world. But that belief wanes through the years. Time takes its toll. Invincibility erodes to disappointment, to doubt, and, finally, to defeat. Floodwaters rise. The light in the eyes dims, and we struggle to understand the point of hope, or the call to persevere. Seemingly stalwart men shift, panic, and sink beneath the dark waters of responsibility, of failure, of loss, of anguish. The world demands all, yet gives nothing in return. As an artist, I had hoped to matter, to be needed, to be noteworthy, to be successful, both commercially and artistically, but ultimately that hope gave way to the acceptance that the work of my hands and mind would, in all likelihood, plunge with astonishing rapidity beneath the waves of trendy, fickle culture. It is a wonder I ever floated at all. I had hoped to make a name for myself, to be of consequence, to rise above the over-saturated marketplace, to surpass ordinary. I sought success with all my rugged heart. But in the end I found disappointment lapping at my toes and, like Peter after his shining moment on the waves, I sank.

Sound. I have listened to the damning voices nearly all my life. They pretend to be holy, but instead of blessing they offer only condemnation, uncertainty, self-doubt, and the firm conviction that I am incapable of bringing anything beautiful or consequential into the world. The voices tell me that everything I do, everything I have ever done, is a waste of my time, of my life, and of the lives of those around me. I fear being myself because the voices convince me that I am a fraud, a phony, a piece of sordid debris adrift in the whelming flood. The odious voices crash cymbal-like in my skull. They assure me that what is broken cannot be repaired. Theirs is noise ad nauseum. Acedia—the noonday demon, the lethargy, the apathy, the cynicism—revels in swamp life. I am prone to wander, Lord, I feel it. Prone to leave the God I love.

The darkness stretches forth for the prone souls: we little half-lights dwelling in our weary states. As post-Eden Adams, we toil at the soil with plastic toy shovels. But the task is too great, the curse too strong. We pull weeds, and they grow back. Tools fail, breaking down in the day-to-day rigors. We yearn for rest, for the work of our hands to be nurtured, fruitful, and blessed. We fight to persevere amid disappointment, amid failure. *Mathein pathein*—we learn to struggle.

Ultimately, in either the end or the new beginning, the secret sadness demands of its prisoner one life for another. It requires an answer. Either life is meaningless, something to be feared and given up for loss, or life is waiting to be *found*, in whatever state of disrepair, and watched over attentively, guarded like the treasure it is.

So I fortify my roots and strain my ears for brighter voices, the voices of friends and family around me—those true saints and angels—and this is what they say: Listen for the breathing compassion of heaven. You matter. Listen to your life. Peel your eyes for solid, dry, true ground; for lasting light; for hope's repair. Churn the waters of discontent; shore up the sanctuary vessel; listen for the trilling birds; let the new year's light bathe the muddy depths, for, as the Psalmist says, "even the darkness is as light" to him who first spoke light into existence.

I try to listen.

The world goes on without us; this much is fact. The darkness creeps in from the brain's recesses, cloud cover-like, reducing the sky to a brooding, grey veil that little to no light or hope can penetrate. In that shadowland, living is an unbearable ache, each breath is a forced sigh. Depression is the wound of a thousand unholy ghosts. But the great and macabre deceit of the secret sadness—the sadness that results in a self-taken life—is that any blessing entrusted to you in your mother's womb is a gift inconsequential, possessing no ability to birth joy or bestow illumination upon another living soul. The lie is that your life does not matter. The lie is that an independent death is preferable to a dependent life. The lie is that the dark burden is yours alone to bear, that being ordinary cannot possibly be extraordinary. The lie is that escape can only be achieved in disappearing below the water's surface, and that the act of walking on water, even racing across it, is a miracle no longer found in the world.

But it is just that: a lie—if only we will unbelieve it.

A stronger voice calls above the storm—bright, fortified, authoritative, commanding the waters. "Come," it says, and miracles answer. The waters part. Faith surges. The drowned arise.

"Even the darkness is not dark to you, the night is bright as the day; for darkness is as light with you."

—Psalms 139: 7-12 (ESV)

"Thus deep into the hill of mole's abode
The reader down and down doth slip
Amazed withal by wondrous word displayed."
　　　　　　　　　　　—John Milton (WNI)

HELPLESS
by Sally Lloyd-Jones

What animal does the Bible say—400 times!—people are most like? Oh dear. It's sheep.

Sheep aren't clever at all. They're foolish!

For instance, sometimes they just topple over and can't get themselves back up again. They just lie there!

And they're constantly falling off cliffs. Or going to unsafe places and getting stuck. Or eating poisonous things. Or getting hurt. Or running off and getting lost. Or not finding their way home again—even if their fold is in plain sight!

So you see, sheep are completely helpless on their own and desperately need a shepherd.

And God says we are helpless on our own too. And we desperately need a Shepherd.

Which is why he gave us Jesus.

"He tends his flock like a shepherd: He gathers the lambs in his arms."

—Isaiah 40:11 (NIV)

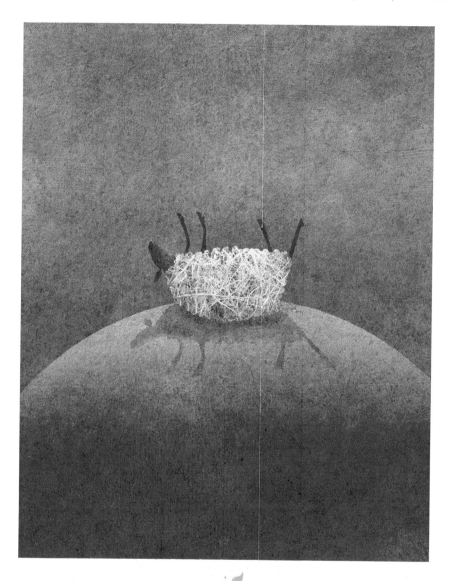

Illustration by Jago

Text © Sally Lloyd-Jones, Illustration © Jago
From the forthcoming *Thoughts to Make Your Heart Sing* (Zondervan)

"In the words of Grundicus the Questionable, 'Seize it, fool! Afore it gets away!'"

—Oskar N. Reteep (WNI)

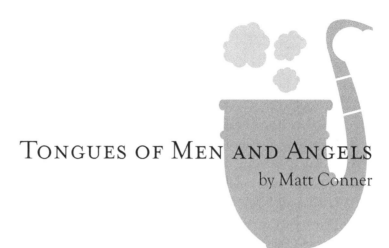

TONGUES OF MEN AND ANGELS
by Matt Conner

N ot every preacher is hot, sweaty and only a prayerful impulse away from lay-
ing a pair of clammy hands on my head, but I'd be well on my way to adult-
hood before I would realize that. At the moment, the clergymen surrounding me
were the same who surrounded us every year at the Circle J Ranch summer camp,
"Where Jesus is Lord." As far as I knew, every Christian teenager at every camp
in every summer underwent the same rite of passage that I was about to endure. I
didn't question it because I'd normalized it. That's what we do. We accept what we
know. The people in our lives, the rituals we practice, the places we inhabit—we
know them as normal everyday life. It's only when we're old enough and experienced
enough to observe other people, other rituals, and other places that we begin to
define parameters for what belongs and what does not. But this particular summer
I encountered a moment that proved difficult to distill.

"How many of you have never spoken in tongues?"

That was the ominous question asked of the two hundred or so students in the
open-air tabernacle. The speaker was a fiery evangelist from N'awlins named Jonas.
He was mesmerizing in every way a hot and sweaty preacher can be. Words with
added syllables. Quiet. Loud. Quiet. Exuding spiritual confidence. Speaking with
authori-*tay*.

"I haven't," I said.

It was true. I had not, up until that night, ever spoken in tongues. I'd seen it all around me in my home church in Southern Indiana where the names of towns like Boonville and DeGonia Springs tell you all you need to know about the region. In my small country church, speaking in tongues was considered a beginner's step. And those who had already taken their first steps were even more spirit-filled: laughing, yelling, running, or fainting. But in all my years, I never took part. I never shook. I never swayed. I never lost control of my words or actions. Yet I also never judged those who did. It was simply normal. It was normal every-Sunday life. They accepted me and I accepted them. No existential questions were asked. No challenges were given. Not until that night at camp.

Once I had identified myself as one of those whom Jonas was asking about, I was encouraged to step out from my rudimentary wooden pew and walk down the hay-strewn aisle to the front of the assembly. After several minutes of hearing the same question again and again, nearly forty of us stood at the front of the congregation.

"Hallelujah! Praise the Lord!"

Everyone was shouting. Everyone was emotional. We were all excited, antici-pating what the Holy Spirit was going to do that night. Then came the hands—the moist, heavy palms that make your head bob four to six inches before your neck can return the pressure with equal force (two years later I diagrammed this while bored in my AP Physics class).

Jonas prayed over us, commanding the Holy Spirit to fill us all with the gift of *Tongues,* while also preaching to the masses that if anyone is a Christian, the gift of *Tongues* is the evidence needed to prove it.

I can't remember the exact words of the prayer Jonas prayed that night. Anyone who uses quotation marks to insinuate that they remember specific conversations is subject to my suspicion, so I won't pretend that any quotes I'm using here are entirely accurate. As Julian Barnes writes, "If I can't be sure of the actual events any more, I can at least be true to the impressions those facts left. That's the best that I can manage." Amen.

Fifteen or more local church clergy, whose youth groups made the trip to Circle J Ranch each year, surrounded us. They were each speaking in tongues to show that they also had taken this spiritual rite of passage. It was safe. It was okay. Look at us. Someday you, too, can pray and preach and anoint. And sweat. It was a Pentecostal reality show and I had suddenly become a contestant.

After being prayed over and instructed on what to expect, several of my peers inside the circle did as they were told. They *spoke*. Some of it sounded ridiculous; some of it sounded like a real language; none of it could I understand or interpret. One girl did a machine gun impersonation and everyone rejoiced. In others, fits of uncontrollable laughter and nervous tics seemed to spontaneously break out. Everyone was convinced, in that moment, that the heavenly chorus was growing stronger as the Holy Spirit moved in our midst.

Looking back, it's obvious to me that it was all planned and carefully orchestrated, but I was blind to that at the time. Naïve? Absolutely. After those kids did their speaking, a few of the pastors moved them aside and told them to "keep going," while the other pastors attended to those of us in whom the Spirit had yet to manifest.

Jonas resumed his prayer, and again the hands landed on my back, shoulder, forehead, and neck. After several minutes, more of us in the circle began to speak in tongues. Again, those students who *spoke* were celebrated and subsequently pushed aside. It was a whittling down to the God-forsaken inner circle.

There was a girl opposite me. I started opening my eyes on the third or fourth pass, and I noticed that she did too. We were somehow not spiritual enough for the rest of them. And we knew it. No matter how many times they prayed, we just weren't feeling it. After five passes, it was clear that they were going to keep going until we were the only ones left. I had only one choice. In a place like that, being obstinate is not an option. Even a polite refusal or a quick I-think-God-wants-to-deal-with-me-back-in-my-cabin-alone would not work. It was clear: I was going to have to speak in tongues.

On the sixth pass, Jonas prayed and preached and delivered with heartfelt conviction his firm belief that God wanted every single one of us to speak in tongues on that very night. Then he gave us the out.

"Sometimes you will think it's gibberish," he said. "You'll feel stupid. But you just need to be obedient and let it out. Just come out with anything."

Up until this point, I had truly been hoping for something spiritual, something sincere. I *wanted* to speak in tongues. I wanted to be included. It's bad enough to stand out when wrestling with adolescence, but in a scenario like this, the last place I wanted to be was inside that circle of outsiders. I wanted both God and personal space—and in that moment I had neither.

I spoke.

"Lotta. Lotta. Lotta. Lotta. Lotta. Lotta."

That quote, at least, I can remember verbatim. For some reason, I decided to use the word "lotta" and say it over and over again. The instant before doing so, I made eye contact with the girl across from me. We both knew that we were making a run for it, so to speak. She joined me, although I cannot remember exactly what she sounded like.

"Hallelujah!"

"Praise the Lord!"

One of the pastors pulled me to the side.

"I knew you'd be a tough nut to crack, but God wants to get a hold of you, young man. It's about time."

We still meet every now and then.

Jake works in a Presbyterian church. Ryan is a Southern Baptist pastor. Chris is obtaining his credentials in the United Methodist Church. I am a church planter within the Christian & Missionary Alliance. We all came out of the same system, the same summers spent together and filled with what we now label as both beautiful and tragic. Decades before any of us were born, a loose network of small, independent, charismatic churches came together and established the summer camp traditions that had defined our spiritual adolescence. The camps were extensions of our home churches, but the experience was intended for a greater intensity. It was intended that we should receive more of God, more of the Holy Spirit, more for the sake of more.

It often amazes me that we're still interested in God, let alone willing to work within the church. While a select few continue to support the same structures we were raised within, the majority ran for the hills and abandoned their faith altogether. A few of us found God on the other side.

There's something sacred about this circle, this fellowship. While we talk about how old our children are, how the years have changed us, and what our ministries are like, we always come back to the same thing, like vultures circling around a subject that continues to define us to varying degrees.

When the movie *Jesus Camp* came out there was a lot of buzz about it. It's a documentary featuring an extreme, one-sided look at conservative, charismatic Christianity. The film captured some elements of that culture that hit very close to home—elementary school children taught to become fiery evangelists, fear-centric religious rhetoric, emotional manipulation. But for me, it was no big deal. It was par for the spiritual course. After all, I'd once called such things normal. Our group discussed the movie and how our specific experiences compared to what it documented. During the discussion I realized that Jake was the only one who hadn't weighed in, and it was clear that the tenor of the conversation was getting to him.

"I couldn't watch any more," he told us. "I saw a clip of the film at a church conference. Someone used it as an illustration and I immediately started to cry. I couldn't take any more. It reminded me so much of camp and I didn't want to go back there."

I found myself moved in that moment. We all did. None of us wanted to "go back there." That afternoon, over lunch and subsequent coffee, we processed our reactions to the film. It brought back memories and forced us to confront them. A few of us were stalled at some level of pain and bitterness. Others expressed the joys of their own spiritual lives as they found freedom and peace after the pains of the past had faded. Together we reflected on the highs and lows of the journey we all take.

We do it every year. We probably always will.

Did you hear that James was shot?

I received that text message three hours after he bled out on the sidewalk.

James had shown up at his church early that morning to let in a group of community volunteers who were coming to clean the attached historical cemetery. He decided to stay and finish his sermon. A few minutes later, an allegedly insane woman walked in the door and pulled the trigger. Three times. At the age of 29, James—the pastor, husband, and father—was pronounced dead from gunshot wounds.

I had attended summer camp with James and his siblings. After high school graduation he attended Bible College, then returned to pastor the church of his youth (the church in which he was eventually shot). I hadn't seen James for several years. Facebook carried on our friendship more than any recent real-life interaction. Yet with so many friends and experiences in common, it was a given that I would go to the funeral. Hundreds of family members, friends, and members of the community of Southport, Indiana, flooded into the megachurch that had volunteered their sanctuary for the occasion.

I made the trip that day to pay my respects to James and his family as well as to connect with old friends. What I hadn't counted on was seeing the faces of the numerous pastors who had so defined those days at summer camp. I felt stupid for not expecting them to be there. James had, after all, been one of them—at least in company.

When the visitation ended, I quickly headed for the back of the auditorium, longing to grab a seat by myself and keen to avoid any unwanted attention. I wasn't alone. Eight other guys were apparently thinking the same thing. We sat in a row, all in a sort of orchestrated display of independence or obstinance. Perhaps both.

Funerals are usually either joyous celebrations of eternal life, replete with themes of heaven and rest, or somber events filled with sorrow and grief. But James's funeral was something in between. Instead of reflecting on the tragic circumstance of burying her son, James's mom spoke of his heart for the down and out. His wife's statement focused on the ebullient joy for the kingdom that her husband displayed to anyone who would listen. Friends described James's life as a ministry "from Southport to South Africa," concerned about issues of poverty at home and abroad.

I wept. I wept at the courage of a mother admitting she felt the void. I wept at the tenderness of a best friend who played James's favorite song. I wept at the challenge and beauty of a brief life well lived.

But I also wept with what I can only describe as an inner violence. From my vantage point on the back row, I might have been safe from some things, but I opened myself to others. Directly in front of me sat the man whom I see most clearly when I recall the manipulative camp experiences of my youth. Other figures from my charismatic past were also strewn about. The last time I had seen any of these men, Driver's Ed had been on my class schedule. Suddenly I was confronted not only with the grief of the moment but with the feelings and memories that those faces were dragging to the surface.

The entire experience jarred me with a force that was difficult to process, even days later. It was an incredible mix of feelings. A complexity of emotion I've rarely felt. The joyful reunion with old friends, the sincere celebration of meaningful life, the communal void left in the absence of James's life, the unwelcome return of unwanted memories. It was, as they say, quite a day.

—⁓—

I'd prayed for healing before, but not while wearing a mask and gloves.

Having grown up in a Pentecostal environment, I've witnessed first-hand some incredible miracles in my life—a middle-school friend's withered hand moving again for the first time, a clinically blind classmate screaming as he began to regain his sight. Those things mark you for life in a strange and beautiful way—through God all things are possible, even if the miraculous seems to rarely happen.

When I became the lead pastor at The Mercy House, I did so through a network of churches all connected to the same "mother ship." Muncie Alliance Church had planted a handful of churches in East Central Indiana, and ours was one of them. Every Tuesday, pastors and staff members came together in a central location for what we called "The Teaching Pool."

Each Teaching Pool consisted of diving into the Scriptures together for a few hours and then grabbing lunch. While we would all end up preaching vastly different sermons, we each worked through the exact same scriptural text on Sundays, and the wrestling match that happened Tuesdays in the Teaching Pool helped shape our views of the Bible in dramatic and meaningful ways. The time also bonded us together as we shared joys and struggles with those who understood the pressures of ministry.

On this particular day, the Teaching Pool group drove out to visit Don, a friend who had been sent home by his doctors to die peacefully. After an arduous battle with cancer, Don's prognosis was that he had precious little time left. He was a pastor and had four teenage children. Don's church was alive and vibrant with new converts nearly every week. His predicted death felt so wrong, and it seemed only fair that God should intervene in some way for a man clearly not done with Kingdom work on earth.

I wasn't sure what to expect as we entered the sterilized house. We put on masks and gloves and gathered around Don, who'd been given a permanent refuge on the living room couch. His wife exited the room and listened through the kitchen doorway as we asked Don about his condition and how he wanted us to pray for him.

"I still believe that God will heal me."

Filled with faith, we agreed with him. We prayed that day that God would heal him. We prayed that Don would get up, even at that moment, and walk away in a New Testament vibrancy of life and spirit. We prayed that God would be glorified because Don would live out a story that only God could author. We went around the circle and gathered as much authority in tone and demeanor as we could muster. We muttered and hummed as others prayed. We concluded our prayers, held his hand for a lingering moment apiece, and then drove back to the mother ship to process it all.

After lunch, we lamented Don's condition and decided to continue to pray for our brother who was near death. Ten or twelve of us gathered, and Guy, a fellow pastor, opened our time in prayer. Then came the silence—an open-ended time for each of us to speak as we felt led by the Holy Spirit.

I will never forget what happened next. My friend Josh was by far the most mystical of any of us in the room. He has a spiritual sensitivity and discernment that I've rarely seen. If I didn't trust him so much, I might have been uneasy with what was about to happen. While we were all silent and uncertain of what to say, Josh found a corner of the room, he lay down, and from that corner he began to speak in tongues. He broke a silence that had lasted perhaps sixty seconds. He broke it with a beautiful, elegant string of words that I could not understand.

In an instant, I was brought back to the outdoor tabernacle from my youth. Yet here the atmosphere was different. Trust was present where manipulation reigned before. Peace was present where emotions once ran high. An experience that could technically be called the same had never felt so different.

Nearly as soon as Josh began, I felt a previously-unknown sensation literally filling me up. It began in my feet and slowly moved up my entire body. It was simultaneously frightening and exhilarating, and I can only describe it as white heat. I remember rocking back and forth ever so slightly as my lips began to tremble. I honestly hadn't the slightest clue what was happening to me, but I knew one thing: I was losing control of my own self.

As soon as Josh finished, I began to speak in a way I had never spoken before. To write down what I said that afternoon would cheapen the sanctity of the moment. I also don't write it down because I spoke in first-person perspective as if I were the mouthpiece of God himself, and I fear I might be struck by lightning if I try to recreate such a thing.

Looking back, I'm a bit embarrassed and humbled by the entire affair. I realized later that what I said was the interpretation of Josh's speaking, and it called all of us to a dependency on God that we had never known before. We were not to pray for Don's healing any longer. Don was in the place he was intended to be, and all of us should only be so lucky to become so dependent upon God.

When I regained control of my faculties, I remember sobbing uncontrollably. It was all I could do. I didn't know what to say after that, and at first, I was too sheepish to talk to anyone for fear of what they thought of my outburst. But after all was said and done, it was clear that God had spoken. We were humbled. Our perspectives had changed.

For me the lesson was a deeper one. It was a significant revelation during my personal journey of learning what it means to believe in something you don't understand. In one story, I was wounded. In another, I was healed.

———

God was not absent during those days at the Circle J Ranch. It took me a long time to realize that, let alone to admit it. It's taken me years to move on from the memories, from events that I could describe as spiritual abuse. But to do that, to move on, I had first to go back.

Initially, I talked myself out of it, believing that it was an unnecessary trip down memory lane, and that it's better to leave such stones unturned. Later, I took it more seriously. I planned to go back to confront old ghosts. But some houses remain haunted for a reason—patiently awaiting their day of exorcism.

Finally, I ignored my nervousness and made the trip. I took the familiar right turn at the only stoplight in Selvin, Indiana—the last town before you reach the gravel road that leads to the dirt road that takes you out to the old Circle J. The name of the camp has changed. Some of the buildings have been restored, but there's no mistaking it—it still has the feel of the old camp days. I drove up the dirt path, past the newly minted sign, and parked beside the flagpole.

The place was, thankfully, empty.

There was the mess hall where I once ate three meals a day and flirted with my yearly girlfriend at the snack bar after evening services. There were the cabins on the right with twenty sagging bunk beds apiece. There was the separate bathhouse where spiders the size of baseballs would lather up alongside you.

There, also, was the tabernacle, an open structure without walls, with a natural slope toward a wooden stage and plenty of altar space. Images immediately flooded my mind. For most of my life, I'd gotten dressed up in a shirt and tie every sticky summer night and sat/stood through three- to four-hour-long gatherings. Old Maranatha! choruses echoed in my head, memories of Sister Judy at the piano playing the same song over and over again.

I sat on the back row and observed for some time. It was likely a purposeful move that I sat in that spot, although I didn't recognize it then. I needed to come back to this place. I needed to take it in again, as an outside observer looking on from the fringe.

Yes, it was here that I was forced to "speak in tongues." Yet it was also here that I truly *felt* the love of God for the first time in my life. The level of my experience at Circle J Ranch was high, intense even, and any sense I have of understanding my personal journey, or the touch of God, hearkens back to those days, to this dusty tabernacle.

I cried as I recollected some aspects of the journey. I laughed at others. I eventually stood up and walked around the tabernacle and traipsed through the rest of the campground, and I realized the paradox of the place. The sign's tagline proclaimed that "Jesus is Lord" here. For a season, I believed that. Then I believed the opposite was true. But on that final cathartic visit, I realized that the sign had been right all along. It was here on the hay-strewn path, on the verge of adulthood, that I had decided to dedicate my life to Christ. It was along the fringes of grass beside the tabernacle that I received the unmistakable vision of my future in vocational ministry. It was at the foot of an old rugged cross, away from the crowds, that I experienced a vision of a life to come—one that has held true through myriad life changes.

Jesus *was* Lord in that place precisely because of the paradox present there. Jesus was present in the beautiful times, but Jesus was also present in the confusing times. No matter what beauty or tragedy life holds—and our stories always include both— the presence of God never changes. While my scars remained, it was nevertheless a moment of healing to realize that the camp in all its paradox was woven deeply into the tapestry of my life. And God, I found, was at the heart of all of it. In the places of pain that are difficult to return to, we are somehow made whole again. It is the swailing of the forest that allows new life to grow after the old is burned away. New wineskins replace the former. The growth that exposes our differences eventually gives way to another that binds us back together.

As I sat on the back row, I prayed for the camp—for the students who would be coming back next summer, for the pastors who return year after year. I prayed for my own journey, that I would not throw away the positive and beautiful things to rid myself of the negative and tragic ones. But most of all, I prayed for my heart and for the hearts of those touched by summer nights spent on this yet-hallowed ground— that they would never become cold or blind to the power and beauty of the kingdom of God as it breaks through in unexpected places and unexpected ways.

It's a prayer I am still reciting.

"To the last page, I grapple with thee."
    —KHAN NOONIEN SINGH, Wrath-Haver (WNI)

BILLY COLLINS AT THE AIRPORT
by Andrew Peterson

You looked as much like Mr. Collins
As you ought to have: bright-eyed,
With a minuscule smile, as if you knew
Something the rest of us could only know
If you put it down in a ten-line poem.
You were putting on your suit coat
After having been undressed
And x-rayed by the security officers,
Who I'm sure had no idea what
You were really smuggling,
Unaware that they were patting down
The thighs and buttocks of a poet laureate,
Searching all the wrong sensitive areas
With their bright blue latex gloves.
They couldn't imagine that they were,
In that moment, merely metaphors
For some wry, lovely, dangerous thought—
Something about windows, or fruit,
Or maybe something even worse.

"In all of art and science there is perhaps nothing I detest more than the absence of a helping of *The Molehill* at Sunday breakfast—well, that and direct current. *Edison!*"

—Nikola Tesla, Wizard of the West (WNI)

THE CLEVEREST IDIOT
by S. D. Smith

I t is popular these days to say you were born at a young age, but I wasn't. While many babies depart the womb as soon as possible, I hunkered down for the long siege. Some call it being dangerously overdue; I call it patience. It works on the same principle as chewing your food the requisite thirty-two chews before sliding it down the hatch. I was, you might say, in no hurry to slide down the hatch into the wide world. "He'll come when he's ready," the nurses said.

Let me steep a while, I thought.

My mother is convinced I was simply over-thinking the birth. It's a habit I never outgrew—not over-thinking births in particular, but over-thinking in general. By Mom's accounting, my indifference to the obstetrician's plan for my life—not to mention my indifference to my mother's misery—was the first sign of trouble.

My father traces my over-thoughtfulness back to the day he first read me that classic of inspirational children's literature, *The Little Engine That Could*. In this era when slackers, hipsters, and scofflaws carry the day, the little engine comes across as overly earnest, perhaps. But I bought in. Just like the stubborn little engine, who wouldn't surrender but bent his mind toward believing he could overcome, I determined to grab hold of the power of thought and squeeze the life out of it. That's what I call transformative literature.

A story from my earliest days, when I was still crawling around on the carpet, illustrates just how important, and dangerous, the power of thought was in my life. My mother's version, I should note, differs significantly from mine. So significant are its omissions and additions, in fact, that I must deem it non-canonical and spare you its heresies. I share with you then, the Authorized Version of the tale—sans Apocrypha.

I was, and I pass this on for informational purposes only, an extraordinarily clever child. But like all children, I had a taste for sweets, brought on at an early age by the generous introduction of a cookie from my older brother, Sidney. One taste was all it took. The pusher had hooked me, but I was quickly cut off by law enforcement. The parental units barred me from such sweets on the dubious grounds that I needed something that scientists in lab coats call "nutrition."

One Saturday morning, not long after the interdiction policies had been put into place, I saw the cookie jar on the table and longed for another taste. I was free to look and to long without interruption or interference because the family was distracted by preparations for my cousin's wedding which was to start in a few hours. Mom was working furiously to finish the alterations on the wedding dress, which she had spread out on the wobbly kitchen table piled high with the clutter of a week given over to wedding preparations rather than housekeeping. There, amid the clutter, was the aforementioned cookie jar, the repository of all my earthly desires.

Mom had to rush out—frantically, as is the custom—and get "one last thing" to complete the wedding dress. As soon as she was gone, Dad went upstairs to see if he could squeeze into his black suit, as he had earlier promised he could. My brothers and sisters scattered, including Sidney, but only after sneaking a few cookies from the jar. There in Sidney's shadow, I stared up with what I can only imagine was a mystifying combination of cuteness and fury. He took a bite of his cookie, then gave me a shrug that said, "I stuck my neck out for you once already, kid. You're on your own."

I was alone with the cookie jar. There was an obvious course of action here: climb a chair and ascend to that higher plane where one achieves the state of consciousness that only forbidden cookies can bring. But I was never one for the obvious course of action. I chose instead to overthink.

At breakfast my mother had once again bemoaned the sad condition of one of the kitchen table's legs. She worried aloud that it would collapse and kill several of us. My father mumbled promises of fixing it as soon as possible but noted that he was presently engaged in the sports page and could foresee no immediate point of disengagement. My language comprehension—while advanced for my age—was imperfect, to be sure; still, like an athletic hobo diving for the railcar, I had caught on. This was all the intelligence-gathering I needed.

I brought all the strength of my two-and-half-year-old arms to bear on the wobbly table leg. It took several minutes' work, but, like the walls of Jericho, the thing came tumbling down.

As the table began to tip, I crawfished to safety, preparing to enjoy the fruits of my labor—the fruits, in this case, being cookies. What I had neglected to consider, and what became apparent to me as the table and its contents rained down all around me, was that the table held things besides the longed-for cookies-in-jar.

The table crashed to the floor along with the cookies, the sports page, three of Sidney's basketball trophies, half a dozen unwashed dishes, a half-eaten casserole, a radio, two pizza boxes, a potted plant, a week's worth of mail, a pitcher of grape juice, mom's sewing machine, thousands of needles that filled the air like arrows at Agincourt, my cousin's previously-white wedding dress, and a worn-out copy of *The Little Engine That Could*. Never were cookies tossed so spectacularly.

My Dad, having heard the crash from his room, flew down the stairs with all the speed and grace of a penguin tangled in a slinky. He burst through the kitchen door, his twenty-year-old suit doing some bursting of its own, and surveyed the wreckage. Spying me unharmed in the midst of the carnage, he almost laughed. Then he spotted my cousin's grape-juice spattered wedding dress, and a look of amused consternation dawned on his face. Finally, seeing Sidney's three basketball trophies in fifteen pieces, his face blossomed into a picture of stern disapproval.

Meanwhile, I was clutching *The Little Engine That Could* in one hand and stuffing cookies into my slobbering gob with the other. Dad swept into the chaos and reached for me. "You can not do this, Benjamin!" he said, scooping me into his arms.

But chewing a fistful of cookies and hugging my favorite book to my chest, I thought otherwise.

—⁓—

By high school, things had changed. I was taller, for one thing. And my habit of over-thinking had grown taller still. I was, in fact, one of the most thoughtful teens Fledge, West Virginia had ever seen. I was dangerously full of thoughts. True, most teens are dangerously full of thoughts—and not always of the most helpful variety. I, of course, had those as well. But unlike most teens, who sat around thinking *some*thing, I thought about *every*thing.

Or, so I thought.

I thought the traps set out for the teens of the world were of no concern to an intelligent person such as myself. I thought I was immune to the troubles that plague ordinary people, because I, unlike them, could think my way out of them. This fantasy persisted with relatively few hiccups—for a while. But soon enough I ran into impediments on the primrose path.

One day, junior year, I stood in the roughly sardine-can-sized gymnasium of Fledge High, imagining the excitement the night's basketball game would bring. I was invested in the success of the game with more than just my mind. Verily, it called on the deep longings of my soul, mind, and strength. It was the last game of the season and my last chance to emerge from a lingering shadow I had lived under for most of my life. Fledge High's winless streak had stretched on for five seasons, and the team had been awful for what felt like millennia.

In utter darkness, a single point of light can be quite striking. At Fledge High School, my brother Sidney was that point of light. The last time the basketball team had achieved victory, my older brother had been the star player. He had led our team to an improbable regular season triumph and had become a sort of legend in our small town. His star was forever positioned in the heavens above Fledge: a bright— and solitary—point of light. As is often the case, this incandescence led him to fall more easily into a series of other successes. Athletic prowess, like a gentleman, opens door after door for you. In my family, and in my town, all my accomplishments were measured against Sidney's, his basketball victory being the peacock's plume in his feather-embellished cap. I needed desperately to find a way to win. Victory, I believed, would unlock every door I wanted to walk through.

It would cause Dad to look at me the way he looked at Sidney.

So I mentally ran through every kind of play, every shot, every steal, every pass (should the unlikely need arise), and every defensive assignment the game might present. I was deep in the midst of profound concentration when the gym door belched open and a dark figure entered, silhouetted by the hallway light.

"Ben," the shape said. "We're late." I recognized the voice. It belonged to Cyclop Sammy Ford. Sammy possessed exactly one-half the usual allotment of functioning eyes, and wore a patch over the useless fraction.

"Late for what?" I asked.

"History."

"I thought that already happened."

"It's happening now," Sammy said. "Fineman said if you were late to class again you couldn't play in the game tonight. Remember?"

Panic. I let it show for a moment, but quickly resumed the cool nonchalance I was known for. The gym was dark so I doubted he had seen my panic-stricken look.

"True," I said, "but Principal Fineman need not know."

"Just come on," Sammy said.

I came on. We ran down the halls to the classroom and Sammy wondered aloud how I planned to extricate us from this particular quandary.

I ticked off our options. "Tell Hatfall we were making copies for Principal Fineman?"

Sammy snorted. "Nobody has let you get near the copier since you—"

"That'll do," I interrupted. "Maybe we could sneak in the room's back entrance."

"That's a closet, not an entrance," Sammy wisely observed.

"Pretend we're on time, and everyone else is early?"

"Hatfall has a clock," Sammy said.

"Fire-alarm?"

Sammy shook his head. "We agreed to save that one for genuine emergencies."

"But we're playing Braxton County tonight! And it's the last game of the season." Sammy didn't need to be reminded just how formidable the Braxton County team was, nor did he have to be reminded that I played a crucial role in Fledge High's admittedly slim hopes. I was a good player, maybe great by Fledge High standards, though we were winless in my era. Sidney's shadow hung over me like a baby blanket and I was anxious to stop toting it around. I wanted to run straight for the fire alarm.

"It doesn't pass mustard," Sammy said. His vocabulary didn't pass muster, but I was glad he was in my company. When one lives in rural Appalachia and one has a vocabulary on the comparatively large side, one is either forever at odds with the world, or one lets things slide. It's bad enough that one says "one" when referring to oneself. Why make matters worse by correcting everyone all the time?

"I guess we're forced into dramatic charm," I said, determined. No problem. I could think my way out of this. I was sure.

"Exactly what do you mean by—"

"Follow my lead," I said and burst through the door.

Mr. Hatfall, the History teacher, was in the middle of a lesson on Geronimo. According to the curriculum, we were studying ancient Greece, but Mr. Hatfall always managed to expound on the plight of the Native American for the full fifty minutes, the curriculum notwithstanding. Teaching this subject—in *every subject*—was like Christmas for him, and he never grew tired of the American nativity scene.

"Misters Gray and Ford, so nice of you to join us," Mr. Hatfall said, flawlessly reciting the line that is apparently taught in every teacher education program in the world.

"Mr. Hatfall! We've been chased," I said, pretending to be out of breath. "In the gym . . . the Hill People . . . hot on our trail. We had no choice . . . ran away . . . led them to . . . anthropology class . . . for study."

"I think you're lying," Mr. Hatfall said, as if detecting some great mystery in some great detective mystery. "We don't even have an anthropology class at Fledge High School."

The class, which was snickering already, roared at this. They were almost entirely in my corner. It must be said—and I offer this strictly for informational purposes—that I was a popular kid. I guess I was the closest thing to a renaissance man that Fledge had. To be sure, the market for renaissance men was depressed in Fledge, but I maintained a sort of charmed popularity. Mr. Hatfall, however, had the look of a man who was up to his ears in renaissance men and couldn't possibly stand another one. "Do you find yourself funny, Mr. Gray?" he asked.

"Not all the time." I said. "But just this instant?" I waited two beats—*one chimpanzee, two chimpanzee*—"No sir. Not funny at all." Peals of laughter.

Mr. Hatfall wheeled on the class with a look of such such ferocity that they all stopped laughing. "I see you do think you are funny," he said, noticing the wry smile I flashed at my fellow scholars. "Well, I do not," he said.

"Me either, sir," said a voice from the back. I didn't need to turn and smirk to see who it was, but I did anyway.

Andy "Moonwalker" McDoogle.

Andy McDoogle was your average redheaded kid of Irish decent, freckled and fair, who had always been an ordinary pain in, shall we say, the back of the class. That is, until last year when he became an extraordinary pain in the back of the class. He had "converted" to Native Americanism. For the previous year he had come to school dressed in what he believed to be Native American costume, feathers and all. He had even unofficially changed his name to "Moonwalker." As you will have guessed, part of this was due to the constant influence of Mr. Hatfall and his all-Indians-all-the-time philosophy of history. The other influence was Moon Jones, the smartest and most beautiful girl in the school.

Mr. Hatfall said, "Thank you, Andy—er, I mean Moonwalker—for your opinion."

Moon Jones stared arrowheads at Andy, who was just happy she was making eye contact with him. He shot up his hand to do an "authentic Native American" salute he had read about recently, but Moon's eyes were back up front where the action was.

She and I, along with Andy, Sammy, and most of the class, had been in school together since kindergarten. Moon and I had a kind of understanding. Or, in any case, I had a kind of understanding. The smartest, most popular boy in school and the smartest, most popular girl in the school were destined to be together. She was, unlike Irish Andy, one-hundred percent genuine Cherokee. She took her heritage very seriously. Andy's conversion and the subsequent "cultural" inquiries distressed her.

"Mr. Hatfall, could you ask Andy not to interrupt class?" I asked, trying to shift his anger away from me.

"I'd like to ask you not to lie to me, Benjamin," he said.

I was going to say that my obvious, deliberate, theatrical exaggeration wasn't really lying, but I settled on something else. "Sir, I was just kidding about the hill people. I know you're too smart to lie to." It was time for direct revelation. "I was in the gym, visualizing our extra-important game tonight with Braxton High. I am really sorry I was late to class. I'd say it won't happen again, but this is History, and we all know what the fellow said about being doomed to repeat it." Mr. Hatfall nodded sympathetically, clearly softening toward me. He was a great lover of clichés in general, and the "history-doomed-to-repeat-itself" cliché in particular, and he was disinclined to takes sides against anyone espousing such wisdom. Things were looking up. Then Andy the Fake Indian played a trump card.

"White man speaks with forked tongue, sir." He thrust his arm in my direction. The leather fringe dangling from his sleeve wagged like forty accusatory fingers.

"You're right," Mr. Hatfall said, pondering these things in his heart "White man *does* speak with forked tongue!"

"Lying?" I said, trending towards desperate exasperation. "Sir, you're listening to Andy "The Fake Indian" McDoogle accuse some one else of lying? Sir, he's whiter than anyone in here. This—and Andy too, incidentally—is, literally, beyond the pale."

"Now," Mr. Hatfall said, a bit confused. "Let's not insult anyone's—heritigical preferences." I knew he was reaching. He had just coined a new P. C. term. I didn't want to be disrespectful to him, but Andy was another matter. Andy the Fake Indian had been getting under my pale skin all year.

"Forked tongue," Andy the Fake Indian murmured again from the back of the room.

I was thinking about how much I'd like to stick a fork in Andy McDoogle's tongue when Mr. Hatfall raised his hand for silence. "I have decided I need to report this incident, this unfortunate business of being tardy for class, to Principal Fineman. I'm sorry to say it, Benjamin, but I think this will disqualify you from tonight's game. You do the crime," he said, pausing dramatically, and looking off into the distance, "you do the time."

He didn't seem too upset. I, of course, was devastated. How would my team compete without me? And how could I hope to escape Sidney's shadow if I didn't even play? The Fledge High Indians would be massacred, along with all my hopes for success in basketball, in school, in life.

Andy the Fake Indian was positively giddy. He let out a kind of war whoop. This was too much for Moon.

"Mr. Hatfall," she said, her searing gaze sweeping over Andy's gaudy, fringe-covered shirt. "Could you please ask Discos-with-Wolves back there to be respectful of my heritage?"

Andy the Fake Indian coughed, then said, "Mr. Hatfall, please continue with your fascinating account of Geronimo. I don't know about anyone else, but I showed up to class *on time* today to learn some history."

A faint hope stirred inside me. I scented blood and winked at Moon, who beamed back at me. I went on the warpath.

"Mr. Hatfall, Moon's right," I said, as if before the bar in the case of *Cherokee Nation vs. Fake Indian*. "I really wish her heritage were respected more."

"It's embarrassing, really," Cyclop Sammy said, joining in on the side of the prosecution.

I charged on. "I mean, if Moon showed up tomorrow in a red wig, dressed like a freckly leprechaun, going around saying 'Top o' the marnin' to ya,' we'd all know she was deliberately making fun of Andy McDoogle's heritage. But he's been at it for a year now with his fake Indian antics and no one will speak up for Moon's people."

"Oh, who will speak up for Moon's people?" Sammy almost sang.

Moon looked out the window with noble concern on her face. She tried to produce the solitary Native American tear, but couldn't quite manage it. It was all she could do not to laugh. As anyone who has tried not to laugh while looking hurt knows, facial tremors can work in your favor.

"Mr. Hatfall!" Andy the Fake Indian shouted, "Please, sir."

Mr. Hatfall tried to calm us down. "All right, class—"

"If everyone in the class got up and did drunken Irish jigs, would that be respectful?" I asked. "Come on class, let's show him how it feels." I motioned for everyone to stand and modeled what I supposed to be an Irish jig as an example. In moments the entire class was river-dancing. Pretend mugs in hand. Pretended inebriation on display. Hope rose once more within me, like a rising, hopeful thing.

Mr. Hatfall tried to speak, but he couldn't get any words out. His P. C. filter had gone berserk and left him verbally paralyzed.

"Mr. Hatfall, please!" Andy the Fake Indian screamed. "This is not fair!"

"See!" I shouted, dancing arm in arm with Moon. "Hurts, doesn't it?"

He howled in protest, insisting that he didn't care a tinker's toot for Ireland, but all his protestations were lost in the clapping, dancing, and general tumult in the room.

I was having a grand time but still desperately working the old bean to come up with a plan to stay in the game. If I applied my mind, I believed, opportunity would knock.

There was a knock at the door.

Ah, I thought to myself, *I ask for Opportunity to put in an appearance and along it comes.* So it was that Principal Fineman entered the classroom accompanied by a distinguished man with silver hair, sparkling teeth, a well-baked tan, and a crisp blue suit. This peculiar specimen was accompanied by what appeared to be a teen-aged version of himself: a lad by his side of like tan and teeth, and likewise blue-suited. The teen copy also sported the silver hair, finely quaffed in like fashion to his aged original. These three all walked into the classroom, which appeared just now to be hosting a dance for inebriated youth of the Emerald Island.

"Mr. Hatfall!" Principal Fineman shouted. A scattering ensued. "Get these students to their seats this instant!" The lunatic Irish sat, and Mr. Hatfall cowered under the wrath of the furious principal. Principal Fineman, it must be said, was a fine man, but even the finest have their limits. And his had, unquestionably, been reached.

"I beg your pardon, Mister—Doctor!—Fineman," Mr. Hatfall said, virtually crouching at the enraged man's feet.

Then Principal Fineman asked what so many philosophers, theologians, scientists, and policemen have asked throughout the centuries: "What is the meaning of all this?"

Hello opportunity.

"Allow me to explain," I said, preparing to deliver a calming salvo of witty charm, thereby securing my escape from the promised punishment. "Mr. Hatfall was simply giving us a stirring look at alternative history. He engaged us in a planned activity to illustrate what classroom education might have been like if history had turned out differently. Well done, Mr. Hatfall. Really, it was genius." I then began an enthusiastic slow-clap, but Principal Fineman motioned for silence.

"Thank you, Ben." He leaned toward the elder of the silver-haired twins. "As you can see, Senator Dill, our teachers in Fledge are creative, outside-the-box thinkers." He eyed Mr. Hatfall sideways as he spoke, as if he might like to place him inside the box and seal it up.

"Very good, very good," the senator said. He was, I would soon learn, a powerful state senator from a nearby county. "I'm certain my nephew Carl will enjoy it here."

Carl Dill, the younger version of the powerful senator from a nearby county, nodded and flashed his oppressively white teeth at us. Moon seemed struck. She lit up as if Carl Dill were the sun and his light had done its work on her. And I didn't like it one bit. She and I weren't exactly dating but, as I said, I understood that we had an understanding. This understanding did not include lighting up when miniature politicians with prematurely silver hair flash their perfect teeth in one's direction. I knew that *I* would *never* be affected by such a maneuver.

If I were being honest, I would have to say that there grew in my usually non-violent heart an intense desire to break most, or all, of those teeth. Instead, I extended a hand—unclenched, by a great effort of will—to the young man and cordially announced, "I'm Ben Gray."

"Sure you are, sport" Carl Dill said, not taking his eyes off of Moon. In fact, as my hand folded into his, Carl Dill winked at her. "So nice," he said, still looking at Moon, "to meet you." He withdrew his hand and made a dismissive motion at me. His manner said, "Run along, boy." I felt like this Carl Dill character wanted me to take his horses to the stables and, while I was there, be a good lad and muck out a few stalls.

"Third time's the charm," they say, and I have no objection to them saying it, but presently, I had the sinking feeling that there stood before me a silver-haired man-child possessing three times the charm I myself owned. He seemed to have far more of the stuff than I could, as Sammy might say, "mustard."

Out charm Ben Gray? Unthinkable. But as was my habit, I did think about it. I retreated to my seat, like a cavalry soldier whose fellows had all been scalped, and I sat down. When I raised my head to peer about, the occupants of Mr. Hatfall's History class were staring, mesmerized, at Carl Dill. He seemed, to my great annoyance, to have cast a spell upon them. The spell seemed to call for girls to goggle and boys to stare with a meek, surrendering deference. I was wounded, sure, but I wasn't about to surrender. I still had the game tonight—if I could manage to swing it—to regain the attention of my peers, including the beautiful ones named Moon.

The principal, the senator, and the teacher had each been saying something or other, but I hadn't heard. I had zoned out. I was brooding over the face of Carl Dill like a dour fog upon a proud lake. When I tuned back in I heard Principal Fineman say, "Well, then he certainly cannot play tonight."

My focus returned in a flash. Panic rose in my throat. "But sir," I said, "it's a grave mistake. I don't wish to toot my own horn, but what will the team do without me?"

"Lose by fifty, instead of forty." Principal Fineman said, silently laughing while holding his stomach in an "I kill me" gesture.

"Not to worry," Senator Dill said. "Carl can enroll today. He's quite the player."

I stole a glance at Moon, who seemed to be thinking, "I bet he is." The desire to connect a fist with Carl's inordinately white teeth became almost uncontrollable. Moon was the last person I expected to be smitten with someone like Carl Dill. Moon was the smartest student in school. How could she fall for this guy?

"I'd be happy to suit up," Carl said, pointing to his chest—as if to indicate himself— "if it would help my team."

My *team?* I thought. *Guy's been here for two minutes and it's his team?*

"I'm sure Coach Lyons will be glad to have you," Principal Fineman said. "Why don't we go meet him?"

"Delightful," said Carl.

The caravan of suits filed out, with Carl Dill waving to the fawning students as if he were on a float at the Rose Bowl parade.

When they were gone, I let go a "Phhuth-tuh," with an emphasis on the "tuh." A mist of spittle accompanied my exasperated exhalation, making my point more salient to the nearby kids. "Can you believe that guy?" I said, jerking my thumb toward the door.

"I believe him," Andy the Fake Indian said. "Seems nice—for one of the oppressors, that is."

"He seemed fine to me," Moon said, dreamily.

I kept hoping I would wake up and find out it had all been a bad dream, a sort of humorous nightmare. I would wake up and play the game, win the game, and get on with a life of successive successes.

But it was all real. Sidney's shadow wore a crown.

That evening the Fledge High Indians, *my* team, went head to head with the Hillbillies of Braxton County High. The Hillbillies, who went by "Hicks" for short, were a dominating team, even when not playing perennial push-overs like my Fledge High Indians. The Braxton Hicks were confident and fully expected to deliver a win. But it proved to be a false hope. Fledge High was without its star player: the thoughtful, but suspended, Benjamin Gray. Yours truly miserable. But our team wasn't alone in losing valuable players. The Braxton Hicks were without their top *seven* players, all of whom were injured in a cow-tipping gone dreadfully wrong.

With only five players left on the roster, one of whom had only one arm, and all of whom were inferior players, we actually had a chance.

I sat on the end of the bench, forcing myself to watch Carl Dill, who was *not* a great player, play lazy defense on the one-armed bandit and hit the jackpot on cherry-picked layup after layup to lead the scoring. This was not how I had envisioned the game playing out. I would have scored a hundred against that team—would have, if only I had spent less time thinking about the game and gotten to class on time.

My dad, who had forced me sit on the bench with the team, sat behind me. And Sidney, whose back must have been killing him from the number of times it was getting slapped, sat beside Dad munching on cookies. At least he had the good grace to avoid wearing his old jersey, a copy of which swung from the rafters above us. Our bench was actually the bottom row of the bleachers, set apart from the other front row seats by a faded orange Gatorade cooler that looked like it could easily have been the original prototype. When Carl Dill was nailing the game-winning free-throws, Dad whispered, "Hey Ben, the Silver Pickle is putting on quite a show out there."

"Nice, Dad," I said. "I see what you did there. Silver hair, last name Dill. Not bad. I hadn't thought of that."

"Good," Dad said. "Stop over-thinking things and just act like you've got good sense. Can you do that for me?"

"I think I can," I said.

The final buzzer sounded and the place erupted. Fledge High had snapped an 83-game losing streak that went back nearly five years, all the way back to the days of Lord Sidney. Carl Dill heaved the ball into the air with a hoot, and his infuriatingly white teeth flashed a triumphant smile. I watched as the ball left his hands and the crowd surged toward him. They lifted him, bore him aloft like an ancient king.

My observations after that are somewhat misty. As if in a slideshow, images of jubilation flashed before my eyes. I saw Moon in Carl's orbit and nearly gagged at the haughty wink he bestowed upon her. I saw Andy "The Fake Indian" McDoogle doing an impromptu war-dance in his full Indian regalia. Though I had not yet walked a mile in his moccasins, I still judged him. I sagged on the bench, trying to console myself as my own community rallied around my new-found rival.

"At least I still have my ability to think," I thought.

Then something struck my mind.

―∿―

I awoke three days later in the hospital. The basketball that Carl Dill had sent sailing off toward the heavens in victory had eventually fallen back to earth precisely on that part of my body wherein my thinking is done. No doubt Carl was used to heaving balls in more atmospherically generous arenas, but our little gym had such a low ceiling that full-court, buzzer-beating heaves at the basket were like long, mildly-arcing chest-passes. The ball he so energetically let fly, promptly struck a beam and ricocheted with grisly effect back toward the crowd, striking me squarely on my round head.

"Well, here we are," Mom said. "Back at the hospital. With you. Again."

"This was our home away from home when we were waiting for you to hurry up and be born," Dad added. I looked up at them as if through a film, one in which the hero is struggling to visually apprehend his surroundings.

"You've sure taken your time coming out of this head injury," Mom said. "Oh, Ben," she patted my face and smiled down at me, "you're the cleverest idiot I've ever known."

Dad leaned over me and cleared his throat. "And that includes her Uncle Eric, who won a scholarship to Harvard but decided to start a Beanie-Baby store instead."

"The cleverest idiot?" I said, though my speech was slurred. "I think—I think I am."

Then something moved in my periphery. I squinted as a swath of sunlight from the window hit my eyes. I blinked, seeing for the first time that Sidney had been there as well.

"Oh, sorry," he said, seeing me squint.

He moved back in front of the light.

"I have scrupulously searched the castle archives for the answer. I have even re-read my own numerous critically-acclaimed writings, hoping I might have inadvertently touched upon the subject in *Roots Run Deep: A Compendium of Leafeater Lore*, *Where the Restless Mangroves Roam*, or *A Brief History of Famous People Eaten by Poison-Tongued Jumping Tortoises* (winner of the coveted Arthur P. Pickelheimer Prize for Acrimonious Adverbs). But alas, to no avail. Reader, I humbly lay the dilemma before your feet: Does this molehill, or does it not, contain a giant? The Lyre-That-Never-Lies may have to be consulted."

—PROFESSOR BARNABAS QUILL, Royal Historian of the Island at the Center of Everything (WNI)

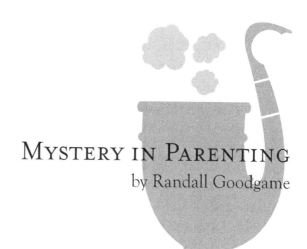

MYSTERY IN PARENTING
by Randall Goodgame

For Christmas last year, we bought a Schnoodle. That's right, a Schnoodle. Go ahead. Try it out nice and schlow. I'm convinced that people started breeding Schnauzers and Poodles just so they could say, "It's a Schnoodle!" And I'm thankful for their cheek, because our Schnoodle, Nilla, is a fantastic dog. If you came to visit, she would smite you with her schnoodly cuteness and eagerness to please. In the first few months of her life with us, her cute factor may very well have kept her alive.

What nearly drove me over the edge wasn't the potty training. And it wasn't the teething or the whining. It was trying to teach Nilla to go on a walk. "Walking the dog" was an absolute misnomer. We should have called it "standing the dog." Nilla would get as far as the front yard, and then she'd stop to explore the landscape one square inch at a time. Meanwhile, my eleven-year-old daughter was a picture of patience and tenderness. She didn't mind the stopping and sniffing and chasing after squirrels, birds, and butterflies, probably because of Nilla's aforementioned cuteness. Once, however, I got so frustrated with all the dilly-dallying that I wound up dragging the poor pup through the grass on her rump before my daughter yelled, "Dad! What are you doing? That's not nice!"

Busted, and grimacing with guilt, I apologized.

A few days later, that same little girl took the leash from the doorknob and clicked it onto Nilla's collar. "Come, Nilla," she said. "Let's go, it's time to walk." When the dog didn't budge, my sweet daughter pulled on the leash and slowly dragged her puppy over the carpet toward the door. Now it was my turn to reprimand, and she quickly apologized—but I felt like the guilty party

Consider the influence parents and children have on one another. Family fingerprints show up in how we talk and laugh, how we argue, how we show affection, how we wound, and how we pray. Most harrowingly, we parents also paint the picture of what "the Christian life" looks like to our kids.

One of the most sobering moments in the Bible happens in Matthew 7, near the end of the Sermon on the Mount. Jesus tells the crowd that they may pray and do great works and have a powerful spiritual presence and reputation, yet still be cast away from his presence on the Day of Judgment if they have not given their daily lives over to the Lord. Yikes.

In that light, if my "Christian life" is full of church-going but doesn't receive the grace of Jesus, seek his wisdom, and submit to his will, not only is my own authenticity in question, but I am a dangerous model for my kids. Instead of introducing them to a living faith, I'm in danger of raising little fakes who proclaim Christ but don't obey him.

A sincere relationship with Jesus, marked by submission to his Spirit, *will* make us better parents. It may seem a little silly to point out the obvious, but if you're like me, you often get it backwards, spending far more time dwelling on how to raise good kids than sitting at the feet of Jesus. But it's the best place to begin, because that's where we come face to face with *mystery*. And I'm learning that embracing *mystery* with my children is like opening a door to a magical room where my faith spontaneously rises to the surface. In that room I recognize my children's deep wonderings as first steps on the sacred journey of the Christian life on which I am both a pilgrim and a guide.

In *Pilgrim at Tinker Creek*, Annie Dillard writes, "We wake, if ever at all, to mystery." As believers in God, we *claim* this life of mystery. We don't know what kind of surprises God has in store hour by hour, so we make our plans in pencil, recognizing that our highest calling is not the working out of our own plans, but is instead a readiness to be available so that God may work out his plan, revealing himself in us and through us. In other words, we listen to an invisible person who inexplicably communicates his will into our minds. It would be right on target to call Christian life the "Mysterious Experience."

As parents, however, we soak our kids in certainty. We say: you may not put your feet on the table; yellow and blue make green; God did not make our house; there is only one way to spell "frog"; a grapefruit never goes in the toilet. To answer and explain is a big part of our job as parents, but we are also to "train up a child in the way he should go" (Prov. 22:6 NKJV), and that way is a mystery shrouded in "clouds and thick darkness" (Ps. 97:2 NIV).

So in between all the certainties of childhood, how do we lead our children in these mysterious ways? The good news: it's familiar territory. Jesus rescued us from our own white-knuckled grip and set us down to walk with him on the narrow path where joy, freedom, repentance, mercy, and forgiveness bloom like wildflowers. The bad news? Explaining this to our kids is about as effective as explaining how to swim while sitting at the kitchen table. The best we can do is lead them out into the water and let them experience it for themselves.

Remember my eleven-year-old daughter? Like most kids, she's been raising deep questions since she was three years old. And whether it's "How do you hear God?" or "Why did God make mosquitos?" my best explanations never satisfy either one of us. In fact, they're usually conversation stoppers, killing the spirit of the question before I know what's happened. So I've learned to stay on the lookout for questions that delve into the mysterious. And I've begun to see many of my children's deep questions as invitations—surprise invitations to experience and celebrate together the great mystery of the Christian life. When I resist the urge to come up with an answer, my child ends up with something to ponder. And pondering is priceless. It is no less than the gateway to the "Mysterious Experience" of Christian life. And *I* get to play a part! We parents get to hold a little hand and follow the trail together into the realm of mystery—right there at the kitchen table.

Practically speaking, instead of giving an answer, I'm more likely to compliment the question and see what she says next. Maybe I'll ask her what she thinks or where the question came from, but my main goal is to acknowledge the reality of the grand mystery. And my hope is that the mysterious way will grow familiar to her in time as well.

Consider this quote from *The Art of Family* by Gina Bria:

> The finest minds, and there have been many . . . have all noted one thing in common: what is spiritual, what is divine, reveals itself. We can't force it, but we can wait for it, watch for it—we can learn how to spot it. And why should we want to do that? Because we are not just physical bodies, physical families, we are spiritual families too.

I need all the practice I can get in recognizing and acknowledging the divine. And every time I engage this way with my children, it diverts our eyes from the shifting sands of a purely materialistic perspective. As the apostle Paul wrote in his second letter to the church in Corinth, "So we fix our eyes not on what is seen, but on what is unseen, since what is seen is temporary, but what is unseen is eternal" (2 Cor. 4:18 NIV). We *can't see* what is *most real!* It is up to us, as parents, to give our children an ongoing context for that kind of thinking. No one else has greater influence or opportunity.

And speaking of Paul, as I begin to dwell on this mysterious life with my children, they begin to recognize Scripture as a relevant and practical source for engaging the deep mysteries of life. I don't break it out all the time, but occasionally one of our conversations will bring a passage to mind, and I'll bring it to their bedside before I tuck them in. Scripture rarely reduces a question to something that can be answered with mere words. Instead, it stirs the imagination and lifts a corner on the vastness that lies beyond our grasp. But this brings me back to sitting at the feet of Jesus. If my relationship with Christ is a healthy one, I am seeking and finding him in Scripture, and the Holy Spirit will have an ever-increasing storehouse of relevant verses from which to draw. Conversely, when I'm not spending time in the Word or in prayer, Scripture rarely comes to mind.

I have seen my own selfishness manifested in my daughter, I have seen my temper mirrored in my oldest son, but I have also seen my wife's honesty and quick wit in both of them, as well as my patience and eagerness to please. We are the rough drafts of who our children will one day become. If we worship the Lord with sincere thanks, the joy of Christ will be familiar to them. If we submit to one another out of reverence to Christ, they will grow into that maturity like they grow into hand-me-downs. If we discipline them with wisdom and love, they will know folly when they see it, and they will more easily recognize true lovers from false ones. But our ability to shepherd them toward holiness depends mightily on our willingness to be sheep.

Am I willing to open myself up to the mystery of the Holy Spirit's leading? In the front yard with Nilla, my own agenda blinded me from recognizing and following my daughter's wise example. I missed out on the joy of the moment and set a bad example for my daughter. With hindsight, I can imagine a different moment—with a wholly different outcome.

I long for my children to engage the deep mystery of their new lives with Christ, but I help them the most when I go first. If my children see me needing Jesus, if they see me looking beyond the resources of the material world for my comfort, wisdom, peace, power, and hope, then I am well on my way to raising up my children in the way they should go. Though the narrow path will always be mysterious to them, I pray that it will also be familiar.

"Moles, moles, moles, moles!
What a world of merriment their melody unfolds!"
                              —Edgar Allen Poe (WNI)

I Come Again to the Woods
(From the Bench at the Bend in the Trail)
by Andrew Peterson

I come again to the woods
To see what might happen.

First it's the sunlight,
Shuffled by fast clouds,
Sifted by bare branches,
To fall, in rolling waves,
On the remnants of green
Shining through the mulch.

Then it's the wind.
It's bending the pages
Of this notebook while I write;
It's hushing the trees
For winter.
Then I notice the absence

Of any bird song,
And I wonder where they are,
And why they're silent
On such a fine morning.

Moondog is on the prowl.
He stopped at the bench
A little while ago
To allow me the honor
Of scratching behind his ears,
Then he trotted off
To patrol the forest,
In which he only shows
Any interest when someone
Is out here with him.

Now a new, distant hiss
Of heavy wind
Sounds on the down
Behind me, charging
Like a rogue wave.
The trees close by are still,
Tensing for the wind's descent.
But the gust changes its mind,
Rattles another grove,
And leaves me and my
Companions alone.
A narrow escape.

(I ignore, in this blessed
forest dance, the racket
of the airplane overhead.)

And God, whose will
Calls forth the winds
Whose patience
Bids the forest
Its winter rest, God—
Who just might speak
To dogs, trees, and birds
More clearly than to fools—
God comes to mind
And I must quiet myself
To listen rather than speak.
Maybe that's what
The birds are doing.

"*The Molehill?* Pfft. Never have I set eyes upon such an intolerable collection of piffle and blather."

—Harmon Bagley, Bagley & Sons Frontier Detective Agency (WNI)

THE STONEMASON'S HOUSE
by A. S. Peterson

A stonemason once lived in a small wooden house near the mountain. He was a quiet man and did not often speak, and because his work required him to wrestle the stones of the mountain, he was also strong. Many of the people in the nearby towns and villages were amazed by his strength and puzzled by his quietness, and they feared what they did not understand.

Though some were puzzled, others said: "Of course he's quiet and strong. He must be strong to heave the great weight of stone. And who would have time to speak with such work at hand?"

It was well that people said such things because they were true. The stonemason loved his work and labored from sunrise to sunset each day.

The people said other things that were true as well—things like "The stonemason's work is the best in the land," and "See what beautiful things he has made of the mountain stone."

And although the people of the nearby towns and villages knew of his quiet strength and of the great beauty of his mountaincraft, no one could recall how old the stonemason was or where he came from, nor could any remember a time when he hadn't lived in the small wooden house near the mountain. They also didn't know that he was lonely.

One winter, a great storm came down from the mountain and covered the towns and villages with snow. The snow was so heavy and the wind so terrible that the chimney in the house of a poor widow collapsed. The widow had no family to go to for help, and she feared that she would die when another night fell because she couldn't build a fire to warm her bones. Though she had no money, and though she feared the quietness and great strength of the stonemason, she went to his small wooden house to plead with him for help. And the widow discovered the stonemason's kindness when he told her that he would come down from the mountain to repair her chimney.

"I have no money to pay you," she said.

The stonemason smiled and told her that she did not need to pay him.

That day he went to the village and repaired the widow's chimney, and when he had finished, her chimney was even better than it had been when it was new. The widow wept and fell at his feet and thanked him. That night the winds and the snow came again, but the widow's house was warm.

The widow was so pleased with the stonemason's work and with his kindness that she told everyone in her village what he had done. For many days afterward, the villagers came to her house to cross their arms and nod their heads and admire the beauty and craftsmanship of the repaired chimney.

Some of the people said to the widow, "You must find a way to repay the stonemason. What he has given you for free is of great value."

The widow thought about this for a long time and decided that it was true. She did not have any money, but when winter ended and spring came, she had a verdant garden. So she labored for a day and a night cooking a worthy meal for the stonemason. She boiled cabbages, she sliced tomatoes, she stewed potatoes, she canned okra, she pickled sweet onions, and she made many special foods that are only known in that small village near the mountain.

She took the food to the stonemason's house, and when he came out to greet her, she was overcome with nervousness. She looked at the ground near her feet as she told him what she had brought and why. And because she was too ashamed to look at him, she didn't see that he was happy she had come.

They went inside, and the poor widow served the stonemason the meal she had made. While she attended him she became more and more comfortable and began to look at his face when she thought he would not see her. She noticed that besides being strong and quiet and very kind, he was also handsome. This made the widow ashamed again, and she kept her eyes to her feet whenever she thought of it. But the stonemason ate everything she brought, and this made the widow smile. When he was done, the stonemason thanked the widow and wished her a good day.

That night, the stonemason was more lonely than he had ever been.

The next day, the widow tended her garden and cleaned her house, but all she could think of was the stonemason. She had forgotten how happy it made her to prepare food and see it eaten. So she cooked a new meal and went to the stonemason's house once more. This time she was not ashamed and did not look at her feet. She saw that the stonemason was happy she had come. As they ate the meal, they talked of many things, and they laughed more than either of them had in many years.

When the widow went home, the stonemason thought to himself that if she came to him again, he would ask permission to court her. And the widow thought to herself that if she brought him one more meal, perhaps there was a chance he would ask for her hand.

She did come to him again and he did ask permission to court her, but their courtship was brief because they were beyond their youth, and they were wise, and they knew that winter's loneliness had ended. The widow and the stonemason were married on midsummer's day.

Many of the people in the towns and villages wondered about their marriage. It was strange to them because no one remembered much about the poor widow except that her husband had died long ago, and no one remembered anything at all about the stonemason except that he was quiet and strong and made beautiful things from the stones of the mountain. But the stonemason and his wife (who was no longer a widow) did not worry about what people said because they lived near the mountain where it was peaceful, far from the towns and villages.

The stonemason continued to work from sunrise to sunset each day. He quarried stone and built beautiful fountains and walls and chimneys for the villages. The widow planted a garden near the stonemason's wooden house and from its produce she made many lovely meals. And though each of their lives continued much as they had before, they were no longer lonely.

The next spring, they had a son. He was strong like the stonemason, but because he was a baby, he was not very quiet. The birth was difficult for the stonemason's wife, who was older than most women who give birth to a child, and as the baby boy grew she was often sick and could not leave her bed. This filled the stonemason with sadness. On the days when his wife was sick, he did not go to the mountain to work the stone. He attended her bedside and brought her whatever she wished, and he cared for his son so that she could rest.

One day while his wife was sick, she called to the stonemason. "I am cold to my bones. Will you bring me another blanket, my husband?"

The stonemason brought her the thickest blanket in the house and covered her in it and kissed her forehead. But when he rose from her side he felt something that he had never noticed before. Cold winter air was creeping through the floorboards of his wooden house. Because he was so large and strong, it was easy for him to ignore the cold and wait for spring. But his wife was not large, and she was not strong. In fact, she was growing weaker every day. When he thought of this, he became angry with himself. His son was even smaller and weaker than his wife (though he was still very strong for a baby). Would the winter cold creeping in make him sick as well?

That night the stonemason made a promise to his wife and son. He told them that he would no longer make chimneys and walls and fountains for the people of the villages. He would still work from sunrise to sunset each day, but his only labor would be to build a new house. Instead of a wooden house through whose cracks the winter cold could creep to weaken them, he promised to build a great house of stone that would keep them safe and warm. The stonemason's wife smiled and thanked him and told him that it was not necessary. But he knew that it was.

The next day, he went to the mountain. The work of a stonemason is slow and methodical and cannot be hurried. With his pickaxe he hewed a great block of stone from the roots of the earth. With ropes and levers and his great strength, he heaved the stone onto his back and carried it down the mountain. The stonemason intended to build a house that would stand for a thousand years. But because the work was so hard and so slow, at the end of the first day he had laid only one stone into its place.

Day after day, he rose and went to the mountain, and each day he returned with a single hewn stone. He laid the stones each beside the other, day after day, season after season.

The people of the villages were confounded. They didn't understand why the stonemason would no longer build their chimneys and walls and fountains, and they came to see what had become of him. For even though some were frightened and puzzled by him, the people loved his work and missed his great strength and his quietness and his mountaincraft.

The people gathered around the site of the stonemason's new house and they crossed their arms and they nodded their heads and they admired the great crafts-manship and beauty they saw.

A few of the people were rude and shouted things at him as he worked. "Why don't you come to the village to build our chimneys and walls and fountains? Isn't that what is required of a stonemason?"

But the wise people of the villages quieted these few, saying: "Do not aggrieve him. Can't you see that he is building a great work?"

No matter what the people said, the stonemason did not look up from his labor. Each day he went to the mountain, and each day he returned with a new stone to place.

While the stonemason built the house, his wife grew weaker. When winter came again the new house was still far from complete and the stonemason's heart was filled with worry for his wife and son. He kept the fire burning in the hearth day and night. He placed stones on the fire, and when they were red with heat he removed them with a metal tong and placed them near his wife's bed. The stones warmed her and kept the winter cold from creeping in.

But she grew weaker still, and at midnight on midwinter's eve, she died. When morning came, the stonemason carried her to a secret tomb inside the mountain and buried her.

The stonemason's grief was heavy, but because his love for his son was strong he continued to build the new house. Each day at sunrise he went to the mountain to work. He carried his son with him in a basket and let him play beside the quarry. Each night he returned with a single stone and put it into its place.

Because of his love for his son, the stonemason was even more determined to build a great house. He knew that he could build a house so strong and so solid that the winter cold could never creep within its walls, but in his heart he hoped to build a house so strong and so solid that not even death could creep within it, and his son would be safe forever. Such a house is built of many stones.

For years the stonemason continued his work, and as his son grew, the stonemason taught him mountaincraft so that he would have a skill. But though the boy was smart, he did not enjoy his work. He learned only what his father required and never took pleasure in what he created. This made the stonemason sad, and his sadness became like a hidden wound that no one could see.

Years went by as the stonemason worked to complete the great house. It was the largest structure that the people of the towns and villages had ever seen. It rose above the trees and towered so high that it was itself like a mountain. It had tall spires and a great hall, and rooms enough to house his son and his son's sons and their sons for a hundred generations.

It was not only large. It was also beautiful. The stonemason had honed his mountaincraft during the years of patient work, and the house was adorned with fluted columns, and wistful statues, and intricate rosettes and flourishes. Great fountains, fed by secret mountain springs, filled the courtyards. There was nothing like it in all the land. People came from far away to see the stonemason's house and marvel at it. They brought their children and pointed to the house said, "Remember this, for there is nothing like it in all of memory."

The stonemason's son, however, did not like to work each day from sunrise to sunset. He often complained, and though his father provided him with food and shelter and everything he needed, he dreamed of the day when he could do as he wished and would not have to listen to his father anymore. He did not understand why his father wanted to build such a house. He could see that his father was old and grey-headed, and he foolishly thought that age had taken the color from his father's wisdom as well as from his hair.

When the stonemason's son was nearly grown to manhood, the stonemason came down from the mountain with a tiny stone, and his son laughed and said to him, "You've worked all day, and this is all you have brought?"

The stonemason laid the small stone in its place, and then he turned to his son and said, "It is finished." The great house towered above them, and the stonemason opened the door and bade his son enter into it. Then the stonemason went into his small wooden house for the last time. He rested from all his years of labor, and that night the stonemason died in his sleep even though he was stronger in his age than he had been in his youth.

At sunrise, the stonemason's son went to the village and told the people of his father's death. They cried out in grief, for the fame of the stonemason had spread across the land and they had prospered from his renown. The people came to the house and helped the stonemason's son bury his father. When the burial was accomplished they stood outside the completed house and marveled at its craftsmanship. But the stonemason's son became irritated at them, and he ordered all the people away.

After the stonemason's death, his son did as he wished. He no longer got up at sunrise, and he no longer worked until sunset. He wandered the halls of the great house and scoffed at his father's folly. After a month, the stonemason's son had eaten all of the food and drunk all of the wine, and he became angry that his father had not stored more for him to live on. He went to the villages and towns and called out to the people from the streets. "I am the stonemason's son. My father is dead and I am hungry."

Some people crossed their arms and shook their heads and grumbled about the boy. But many others took pity on him and brought him food because they honored his father who had been so kind and quiet and strong.

The stonemason's son took the food and ate it in the street and threw what he did not like into the gutter. Each day he went to a different town and called out to the people from the streets. And each day fewer and fewer people took pity on him, until one day he called out for food and none of the people had any pity left. He cursed the town and went away hungry. He went to other towns and villages, but no matter where he went, no one would have pity on him and he cursed each of them saying, "My father made your fountains, and walls, and chimneys, and this is how you repay him? Though I am his son and know the secrets of his craft, I will never mend what he has made for you, nor bring you anything of stone from the mountain."

And so he went back to his father's house and was hungry and angry.

When the stonemason's son had not eaten for many days, a stranger from a far away land came to admire the stonemason's house. The boy threw open the window and intended to shout at the stranger and send him away, but then he had an idea. He told the stranger that the price for looking on the great house was a copper coin. Because the stranger had traveled far and was overcome by the beauty and wonder of the stonemason's house, he withdrew a coin from his pouch and laid it upon the doorstep. And from then on, whenever travelers came to admire his father's house, the stonemason's son charged them a coin, and because of his father's great fame, he soon had enough coins to purchase food and wine and no longer went hungry.

Some people remembered the kindness and quietness and strength of the stone-mason and knew that he would never require money for another to look upon his work. These people went out to the stonemason's house and cried to his son, "You dishonor your father and your father's house!"

The boy was angry when he heard this, and he broke off a piece of stone from the house and threw it at the people.

When winter came, few people traveled the land and even fewer of those came to admire the stonemason's house. Because so few had come, the stonemason's son had very little money and once more became hungry. He went into the village and shouted to the people, "I am the stonemason's son and will repair your chimneys and walls and fountains if only you will feed me." But the people crossed their arms and shook their heads and remained silent because they had learned to repair their own stonework, though their craft was crude and without beauty.

The next day a stranger came to marvel at the house, and the stonemason's son was anxious to take his coin. But he knew that a copper coin would not buy enough food to feed him for the winter, so he told the stranger that the price was a silver coin. And because of the great craftsmanship and beauty of his father's house, the stranger agreed.

When the people of the village learned what the stonemason's son had done, they were even more angry than they had been before. Many came out and stood near the house and shouted at the boy, "You dishonor your father and your father's house!"

The stonemason's son was filled with hatred for the people, and he broke off another piece of his father's house and threw it at them. But they continued to cry out, and he broke off another piece and threw it also. After he had thrown many stones, the people went away.

In time the boy became rich because of his father's fame, but though the house required many repairs from the stones he had broken off in anger, he did not work to repair them. Instead, he spent his coins on food and foreign wines and paid people of poor repute to come to his father's house and drink with him. These people whispered in his ear and slipped their hands into his pockets and advised him that he should demand a gold coin for each traveler come to see the marvels of his father's house. Although the stonemason's son already had enough money, he was greedy and did as they told him.

That winter a great storm came down from the mountain, and because the stonemason's son had broken off so many pieces of the house, the cold crept in and he was often sick. The people of poor repute continued to eat his food and drink his expensive wine, but they did not comfort him in his sickness, and because he was too weak to do so himself, he ordered those in his house to throw stones at the people who cried against him. They used his father's hammer and his father's pickaxe to break great pieces of stone from the house, and they laughed as they hurled them at anyone who came near.

When spring came, the infamy of the stonemason's son had spread across the land. People in every town and village knew of the stonemason's broken house, and they knew of his son who threw stones. No one at all came to pay a golden coin, and no one marveled at the once-great house. But the stonemason's son had become rich on his father's renown and did not concern himself with the next year's winter. When autumn came, however, his wealth had dwindled and all the foolish people of his house had gone away. He was alone and began to worry. So he went into the village and cried out that he would no longer charge a golden coin for people to marvel at his father's house. Instead he would once more charge only a copper coin. But the people of the village ignored his cries.

He was angry with the people but he also feared the winter, and so he went again to the village and cried out: "Only bring me food for the winter and you may come and see my father's house."

But the people crossed their arms and shook their heads, for all their pity had been used up. The boy cursed the village and spent the last of his coins to buy what food he could.

That winter, another great storm came down from the mountain. The snow fell so heavily and the wind blew so terribly that many houses collapsed and many villagers died of cold because there was no stonemason to repair their homes. But though the stonemason's once-great house was pierced with holes and ragged with neglect, it held beneath the great weight of the fallen snow and was stalwart in the gale of mighty winter winds.

The stonemason's son tried to keep warm when the winter cold crept in, but he was often sick. By midwinter, he had eaten all of his food and was near death with hunger. He scoured his father's house for something to eat but found nothing, and his heart was full of hatred for his father and for the people of the village.

One night, in a fever of sickness, the stonemason's son was so hungry that he thought he could eat even a stone. He crawled from his bed and seized a stone in the wall. But such was his father's craft that the stone held fast. The boy took up his father's pickaxe and swung it upon the stone. He cursed his father for building such a house and swung the axe at the stone until it was loosened in the wall. Then, trembling with sickness and hunger, he plucked the stone from the wall to eat it.

But before he could put it to his mouth, the once-great house shuddered beneath the heavy snow and quaked in the howling winter wind and collapsed with a terrible sound that people in all the towns and villages heard as they lay in their beds.

The trembling of the stonemason's house caused the snow of the mountain to break loose and rush down the mountainside. The avalanche buried the stonemason's son and the house and everything in it.

The next day, because of the tremendous sound of the collapsing house and the avalanche, people came from all the towns and villages to see what had happened. Many were glad that the stonemason's son was dead. Many recalled his unkindness and his greed and his laziness. Others remembered how great and wonderful the house had been, and they were sad that it was destroyed and its beauty lost. They looked upon the ruined halls and marveled at all that had happened and said to one another that the boy had brought calamity upon himself and all around. And they returned to their homes, and with crude craft they repaired their chimneys and their walls and their fountains and soon forgot all they had seen.

But a few, only a very few, walked among the fallen spires and smiled and remembered the stonemason and his great strength and his quietness and his kindness. And these few, these very few, said to themselves: "Remember him, for there is none like him in all of memory." Then they took up the fallen stones and carried them away, and they built of them new towns and new villages, and they sought the secrets of the mountain, and they dwelt in the memory of the broken house.

RESTING AND RELYING
by Sally Lloyd-Jones

Resting and Relying
    When you were little, did someone big ever carry you? Did you rest your head on his shoulder, lean your whole weight on him?

Faith is leaning your whole weight on God. Resting your head on his shoulder.

Faith means resting—relying—not on who we are, or what we can do, or how we feel, or what we know.

Faith is resting in who God is and what he has done.

And he has done EVERYTHING.

"And so we know and rely on the love God has for us."

—1 John 4:16 (NIV)

Illustration by Jago

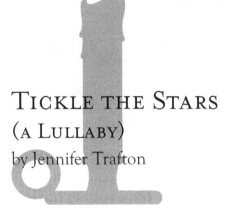

Tickle the Stars
(a Lullaby)
by Jennifer Trafton

Tiptoe to the stars tonight and tickle them until they fall,
and I will catch them in a jar to wink and blink like fireflies.

Put the jar of stars upon your windowsill and blow a sigh,
and I will summon all the shadows to a magic midnight ball.

Grab a shadow's hand and dance and whirl and dive and swirl and spin,
and I will play the tambourine until my fingers dance alone.

Take my tambourine and teach the creatures in the clouds to sing,
and I will hush their cloudy roars and hum into their dragon-dreams.

Clutch a dragon's wispy tail and swing . . . swing higher! . . . now let go,
and I will catch you as you fly and put you in a paper boat.

Sail the paper boat until you reach a castle made of glass,
and I will leave a gift for you: a silver key within a kiss.

Turn the key inside the lock and see a secret sunrise burst,
and I will take the colored threads and weave a little golden horse.

Ride, ride the golden horse around the world and back to me,
and I will shoo your fears away and keep the darkness locked up tight.

Kiss your golden horse goodnight, then chase your jar of stars back home,
and I will love you deeper than the moon can dive into the sea.

Tuck the moon beneath your chin and curl your heart against my own,
and I will love you longer than it takes a star to fall asleep.

Illustration © 2012 Jennifer Trafton

CONTRIBUTORS

RON BLOCK, along with his banjo and his mustache, add up to one fifth of the legendary Alison Krauss and Union Station (our favorite fifth, in fact). He also happens to look suspiciously like G. K. Chesterton. We admire him for both of these reasons. *(www.AlisonKrauss.com)*

DON CHAFFER is a bearded poet/singer/songwriter/producer/composer who has written and recorded more than fifteen albums either solo or with his band, Waterdeep. He's also written two musicals (in his spare time). For his next trick, he intends to ask for a day off. *(www.Waterdeep.com)*

SARAH CLARKSON is the author of *Read for the Heart*, a guide to a healthy reading life for families, and *Journeys of Faithfulness*, stories of life and faith for young Christian women. She hails from the dappled foothills of Colorado and plans to write at least one great novel before she dies. In the meantime, she studies literature (at Oxford) and writes about the wondrous world of children's stories. *(www.ThoroughlyAlive.com)*

EVIE COATES is an accomplished visual artist, a teacher of art to young minds, a culinary wizardess, and an appreciator of many things both strange and wonderful. *(www.EvieCoates.blogspot.com)*

MATT CONNER is a freelance writer. He lives in Anderson, Indiana, and has interviewed nearly everyone who has ever played music. That isn't entirely true.

JUSTIN GERARD is a freelance illustrator from Greenville, South Carolina. He's worked with everyone from Disney and Warner Bros. to Penguin and Harper Collins. When he isn't drawing, he enjoys tank battles and chocolate chip cookies. *(www.JustinGerard.com)*

RANDALL GOODGAME has recorded eight albums including *War & Peace* and *Bluebird* as well as children's albums such as *Slugs & Bugs Under Where?* and *A Slugs & Bugs Christmas*. He cannot fly or use Excel, but he can juggle and french-braid, though not at the same time. *(www.SlugsandBugs.com)*

GONZO is a purplish, crookedy-beaked something-or-other of indeterminate origin. He rides a motorcycle, catches cannonballs, and visits Nashville once each year in the fall, where he hopes to find his people, woo Camilla Chicken, and proclaim: "I shall now eat a rubber tire to the music of *The Flight of the Bumblebee*. Music, maestro!"

JASON GRAY is the singer-songwriter of four albums including *A Way to See in the Dark*, *Everything Sad Is Coming Untrue*, and *Christmas Stories: Repeat the Sounding Joy* (coming 2012). He's also one of the shortest men in Minnesota (but don't tell him we said so). *(www.JasonGrayMusic.com)*

LANIER IVESTER is a "Southern Lady," in the best and most classical sense, and a gifted writer, in the most articulate and literal sense. She also hand-binds books and lives on a farm with peacocks, bees, sheep, Margaret Mitchell's bathtub, and the Governor of Ohio's leg. We like her. *(www.LaniersBooks.com)*

JAGO arrived on Earth with a burning ambition to be Superman, Indiana Jones, or quite possibly King Arthur. Afer a little hard work and an awful lot of drawing, he settled on his fourth choice of career: illustrating children's books. He lives in a slightly damp wetsuit in Cornwall with his fantastically lovely wife Alex, beautiful daughter Lily Peach, and small round son, Rudy. *(www.JagoIllustration.com)*

SALLY LLOYD-JONES is a British-born children's book writer who moved to the States in 1989 "just for a year or two." We haven't let her go home yet. While here, she's written a plethora of wonderful books such as *The Jesus Storybook Bible*, *Song of the Stars*, and *Thoughts to Make Your Heart Sing*. We're glad she's still here because neither Hutchmoot 2011, nor this book, would have been complete without an English accent. *(www.SallyLloyd-Jones.com)*

THOMAS MCKENZIE is the inimitable host of the One Minute Review and the pastor of Church of the Redeemer in Nashville, Tennessee. Also, he has samurai swords. We highly recommend this priest. *(www.OneMinuteReview.com)*

ERIC PETERS is a singer-songwriter who has recorded six solo albums including *Chrome* and *Birds of Relocation*. He's also a painter, a curmudgeon, a lawn connoisseur, and a hopeless bibliophile. *(www.EricPeters.net)*

A. S. PETERSON is the author of the Revolutionary War novels *The Fiddler's Gun* and *Fiddler's Green*. He's also the managing editor of Rabbit Room Press and is a nefarious puppeteer who lurks in the shadows, pulling strings and planning Hutchmoots. *(www.FinsRevolution.com)*

ANDREW PETERSON is the proprietor of the Rabbit Room and the singer-songwriter of more than ten albums including *Light for the Lost Boy*, *Counting Stars*, and *Behold the Lamb of God: The True Tall Tale of the Coming of Christ*. He is also the author of the Christy award-winning Wingfeather Saga. *(www.Andrew-Peterson.com)*

TRAVIS "THE HALF-BLOOD" PRINZI, proprietor of TheHogsHead.org, is one of the world's foremost Harry Potter scholars. He even has big words like "blogengamot" to prove it. He's also the author of two books and the editor of *Harry Potter for Nerds: Essays for Fans, Academics, and Lit Geeks*. *(www.TheHogsHead.org)*

RUSS RAMSEY is the author of *Behold the Lamb of God: An Advent Narrative*. He is a pastor at Midtown Fellowship in Nashville, Tennessee, and he remains bravely unapologetic in his appreciation of baseball, floating tremolo systems, and Dutch painters.

JONATHAN ROGERS is the author of seven books including the Wilderking Trilogy, *The Charlatan's Boy*, and *The Terrible Speed of Mercy*. After a notably painfully delivery, he is also the proud father of exactly one short story. *(www.Jonathan-Rogers.com)*

S. D. SMITH exists at the lonely crossroads of strange and wise, and is the proprietor of the Story Warren website. He claims that P. G. Wodehouse is his great uncle on his mother's side, but we don't believe him. *(www.StoryWarren.com)*

JENNIFER TRAFTON is the author of *The Rise and Fall of Mount Majestic*, a nominee for the 2012 Volunteer State Book Award. She hopes to live in Oz and ride a flying monkey to work, but the Immigration Department has not yet approved her visa. *(www.JenniferTrafton.com)*

WALTER WANGERIN, JR. is the National Book Award-winning author of *The Book of the Dun Cow*, *Ragman & Other Cries of Faith*, *Letters from the Land of Cancer*, and many other fine books that we haven't the space to list here. He is also well-known for blowing minds as the keynote speaker at Hutchmoot 2010. *(www.WaltWangerinJr.org)*

The ——

RABBIT ROOM

www.RabbitRoom.com

———

Also available:

Real Love for Real Life
by Andi Ashworth

Monster in the Hollows
by Andrew Peterson

Behold the Lamb of God
by Russ Ramsey

The Cymbal Crashing Clouds
by Ben Shive

The Fiddler's Gun and Fiddler's Green
by A. S. Peterson

RABBIT ROOM
—— PRESS ——